VINTAGE

HALLOWEEN
COLLECTIBLES

MARK B.
LEDENBACH

An Identification and Price Guide

Published by

krause publications
An F&W Publications Company

700 East State Street • Iola, WI 54990-0001
715-445-2214 • 888-457-2873
www.krause.com

Please call or write for our free catalog of publications. Our toll-free number to place an order or obtain a free catalog is 800-258-0929, or please use our regular business telephone 715-445-2214.

All photography by Patrick Satterfield or

Martin Smuts Photography

2014 9th Street, Suite B

Sacramento, CA 95818

(916) 362-8080

Library of Congress Catalog Number: 2003101341

ISBN: 0-87349-562-4

Editor: Jodi Frazzell
Designer: Jamie Griffin

DEDICATION

To Barbara Smuts, the Godmother of my collection!

ACKNOWLEDGMENTS

A book like this, enabling me to share a portion of my collection with those unable to see it in person, has long been a dream of mine. Pulling it all together, however, has certainly not been a solitary endeavor. I have been able to discuss the merits, ferret out the history, and assess the relative scarcity of many of the pieces shown herein with others who toil under the same pleasurable addiction of collecting and/or dealing in vintage Halloween memorabilia. I have enjoyed many hours of conversation with the following folks in the years since my wallet has been overtaken with the acquisition of these items, which hearken back to a more visually interesting autumn era. Many thanks to Carrie Beermann, Ginny Betourne, Grace Caracci, Mark Craven, Sandy Donahue, Leila Dunbar, Dolph Gotelli, Cindy Grew, Mike Hager, Stacey Heffernan, Bobbie Lasky, Hugh Luck, Suzon Martin, Richard Miller, Brian Moran, John Nausieda, Claudia Normandin, Jim Pollowitz, Tim Sedlack, Barbara Smuts, Greg Spatafore, Chris Sullivan, Jason Walcott, and the myriads of others with whom I have been fortunate to interact on the never exhausted topic of Halloween memorabilia! I'd like to especially thank Matthew Kirscht, an incredibly talented artist as well as an avid Halloween collector with an astonishing encyclopedic memory for pricing. His help with this book has been invaluable and generous. I am truly lucky to know him.

Acquiring these items is one thing, but having them photographed professionally, so that I may share my collection with those of you perusing this book, is another thing altogether. The bulk of this key work was done by the ever-diligent Martin Smuts, while others were taken by Patrick Satterfield. I'd like to thank them both for their excellent photography, which is the heart of any collecting reference book.

Putting all of the pieces together into a pleasing format is another formidable task. Thanks to the superb work of Krause Publications, this book should visually keep your interest and perhaps whet your appetite for adding to your own collections.

TABLE OF CONTENTS

HALLOWEEN TRADITIONS IN THE USA

The antecedents of Halloween in the wider world are somewhat murky. Well over a thousand years ago, ancient peoples like the Celts celebrated the end of the harvest season in practices that had definite religious connotations. Beginning in the 1550s, All Saints Day was observed on November 1, with the night before, October 31, thought to be the night the dead returned to be venerated. Over a long time period, this "All Hallows Eve" celebration came to be known instead as "Halloween." These celebratory events were introduced into the United States primarily by the many immigrants from England, Scotland, and Ireland.

It's important to note that Halloween, as celebrated in the United States, had little to no religious connotation, something that is true to this day.

Once these traditions jumped the Atlantic Ocean, Americans remade the holiday into something unique, with the emphasis decidedly moving away from Halloween's original agricultural roots and toward an opportunity to celebrate the autumn season with friends and family. This happened over time. Although Halloween imagery was only sometimes seen before 1900, by the first decade of the new century companies were printing postcards for this "new" holiday and books were being published containing songs, poems, and even plays about Halloween. By the second decade of the 1900s, party decorations were being professionally manufactured and purchased. However, Halloween—as a commonly celebrated event—came into its own in the very late teens and early 1920s. Parties were all the rage then, but these were not for children. They were adult oriented, with guests settling in to play mahjong, bridge, and other games. Tables and walls would be gaily decorated with a wide array of Halloween-themed items, setting the party's mood. The games' winners would be given prizes to take home, like candy containers, nodders, lanterns, or noisemakers. Only later did the more child-focused tradition of "trick or treating" come into vogue as a substitution for the petty vandalism that preceded it. It was at this time that Halloween became inexorably linked with children.

Keep this firmly in mind when looking at the imagery common from this time. Although many table decorations were cute (the 1923 Beistle party set for example), many diecuts, candy containers, and lanterns were pretty scary. This aggressive use of imagery, which is anything but benign, makes more sense when there is a realization that the items were meant to be used at adult gatherings.

Halloween, once adapted to the United States, became a quintessential American holiday, although many of the items most prized today were manufactured in Germany. After World War I, Germany was devastated by the follies of its own policies and hampered in its recovery efforts by the Versailles Treaty. This treaty had many provisions that restricted the development of basic industries, while at the same time forcing the Germans to make reparation payments for the damages caused to the victorious allies during the war. Under these circumstances, several American discount-merchandising magnates like Frank W. Woolworth and Sebastian S. Kresge encouraged German artisans to use their creative expertise to craft unique and wondrous paper items for export to the vast and growing American holiday market. What I consider to be the zenith of German Halloween production in terms of variety and design runs from about 1920 until 1935, when the expansive tendencies of the German Third Reich brought this kind of trade to a close, not to resume until the later 1940s. We shouldn't think of the German **production** of Halloween memorabilia from this era in modern terms. Many, if not all, of the lanterns, candy containers, diecuts, nodders, and figurals were made in homes or very small firms, from either a fixed design or a mold, and all were hand decorated. The overall quantity of items produced was quite small given the conditions present at the time of their creation.

COLLECTING HALLOWEEN

I stumbled wide-eyed into the world of collecting vintage Halloween memorabilia in the late 1980s. I was browsing in a local store, Blue Eagle Antiques, when its proprietor (also my friend) asked if I would help her move several boxes from a back storage area that contained old Halloween decorations for her seasonal displays. Being curious, I opened the boxes and was dazzled by the strong imagery of those vintage pieces. I had never really seen anything like them before. Instantly hooked, I recall writing a check for nearly $350 that day, which bought quite a lot from those boxes! Among my first purchases was the complete set of eight Beistle black cat diecut band members with the HE Luhrs' mark for a total of $16. Those were indeed the days!

I was fortunate to have started collecting Halloween when I did. This "Golden Age" of relative plenty, coupled with low prices and quizzical looks from shopkeepers when asked about the availability of vintage Halloween in months other than October, lasted until about 1995. Being an enthusiastic and passionate collector, I was able to amass a nice assortment of material during this interlude. It didn't seem so at the time, but looking back, prices were at their very bottom. (Talk about market timing!) Starting around 1991, dealers specializing in holiday items emerged, and articles touting vintage Halloween memorabilia began to appear in collecting magazines. Then, in 1995, two references devoted solely to Halloween collectibles were published. The first was *Halloween in America* written by Stuart Schneider. The second was *Halloween Collectables* written by Dan and Pauline Campanelli. Both were informative works written by collectors for collectors. Once these were published, prices truly exploded.

The main factor behind the swift rise in prices for vintage material was the true scarcity of display-quality items. Unlike Christmas decorations that almost always became heirlooms to be carefully packed away as the New Year dawned, Halloween decorations were generally used once at a party and then discarded with no sentiment. Lanterns were designed to be illuminated by a flame that either consumed the lantern or made it undesirable for further use or display. Diecuts were often affixed to walls with liberal use of tape, which through the years causes damage affecting display-worthiness. Games were designed so that in the playing of them, game pieces would be torn from backing or cut away. Party table decorations would be scooped away by a tired host and thrown in the trash. Consequently, there is a true scarcity of quality, near-mint condition, vintage Halloween memorabilla.

The focus of my collecting efforts has been to find superb examples of games, lanterns, shades, candy containers, figurals, nodders, candles, table decorations, party items, noisemakers, and diecuts. I have striven to buy only those items in superior condition and have taken care in ensuring that I preserve them for future collectors.

Taking care of your collection

As with most anything else, light and dust are the main culprits in the degradation of vintage Halloween items. Control the lighting as much as possible and keep your most precious objects in cabinets, which tend to remain relatively free from dust. Try as often as possible to wear cotton gloves when handling your items so as to prevent any oils or dirt on your hands from soiling them. Being admittedly even more extreme, the greater control you exercise over the humidity and temperature variations in your display areas, the better your items will withstand the unavoidable ravages of passing time. Never be tempted to repair an item using cellophane tape. There are few substances more harmful to paper-based products than this.

Dating your items

Accurately deducing the manufacture date of Halloween items is not easy. There are six main ways to do this, which I'll list in approximate order of ascending exactness: looking at the imagery; becoming familiar with how imported products were marked; becoming familiar with the marks used by domestic manufacturers; perusing vintage catalogs from wholesalers; perusing vintage catalogs or other references issued by retailers; and being familiar with the evolution of the United States zip code system.

The imagery of vintage Halloween items through the 1940s is compelling and memorable because it is significantly at odds with imagery common today. The hierarchy of imagery has always been fairly logical: The pumpkin, or its more humanized incarnation, the Jack-O-Lantern (hereafter abbreviated as JOL), forms the bottom of the pyramid as the most common image. Ascending this pyramid, the middle layers encompass black cats, witches, skeletons, and owls. The upper-most layers consist of ghosts, veggie people, and bats, with the pinnacle surely being occupied by devils. This means that within any given genre, devil imagery is the rarest. Although not always true, this rarity generally means that devil imagery commands very high prices. The imagery from this era was meant to unsettle adults. As the 1940s gave way to the 1950s, Halloween imagery was toned down, since manufacturers wished to appeal to the broadest market possible. From that time through today, cuteiness has dethroned subtlety. Today's Halloween imagery, aimed at still broader markets, is by and large, cute, non-threatening, and dull. The rise of chain merchandisers content to peddle the most innocuous material has accelerated this trend. Therefore, one rule of thumb I use when evaluating a piece is this: the scarier or more complex the imagery, the older the item.

The markings used by exporters and some domestic manufacturers provide solid clues to dating items. Talking about imports first, regulations governing how imports were to be marked started to tighten in 1933. Prior to this time, most things were merely marked "Germany" or "Japan," for instance. After this date, a minimum marking of "Made in Germany" or "Made in

Japan" was required. Keep in mind that some items imported prior to 1933 could conceivably be marked "Made in…" since such marking would exceed the then-minimum marking requirements. Also, some items imported after 1933 did use the same molds with the original markings, but complied with the new regulations by affixing a paper label with the now-required marks. Since most, if not all, of these labels are long gone, this gives rise to the very real possibility that modern day collectors could wrongly think they had an item made prior to 1933 based solely on the mark itself. I point out these possibilities to give you an idea of the pitfalls in trying to date imported items merely by the mark. By and large, the simple rule of 1933 should generally suffice when attempting to date these items.

Sometimes a "D.R.G.M. Germany" mark is seen. The initials stand for Deutsches Reichs-Gebrauchs-Muster, which means "German Federal Registered Design." This mark was used in Germany from June 1891 through early 1945, and then only on items that had more than a decorative purpose. For instance, you might find this mark on a lantern or candy container but not on a diecut. The bottom line for Halloween collectors is this: If you own a piece that bears an authentic "D.R.G.M. Germany" stamp, it means that the piece was almost certainly made during or prior to 1935.

After WWII, the marks became more specific. Japanese items were marked, "Made in Occupied Japan" (or some close variant) from 1945-1952. German items were marked "Made in US Zone Germany" or "Made in USSR Occupied Germany" (or some close variant) from 1945-1949. German items made after 1949 would bear a number of different markings, such as "D.B.G.M." (Deutsches Bundes-Gebrauchs-Muster), "Container Made in Germany," or "Western Germany".

For domestically produced items, the marks used varied by manufacturer. (For an overview of the marks used by manufacturers of tin litho items, please see Noisemakers.) For paper Halloween products, the premier American diecut and party supply manufacturers were the Beistle Company of

Shippensburg, Pennsylvania and the Dennison Manufacturing Company of Framingham, Massachusetts. Both are still in business today.

Beistle was more diligent about using different marks as the years passed. Founded in 1900 by Martin Luther Beistle, the company began slowly serving the growing Halloween decorations market in the teens. By the early 1920s, it began producing an astounding variety of fabulous items. The earliest items were simply marked "The B Co." These items almost always pre-date 1920. The next mark seems to be "The Beistle Company" printed in small letters with no copyright symbol present. Their diamond mark was used from about 1925-1930. This is a diamond with the word "Beistle" in the center with the words "Trade" above and "Mark" below and enclosed within the diamond. "Made in U.S.A." appears beneath and outside of the diamond. Beginning about 1939 and continuing through the 1950s, many Beistle products were marked "HE Luhrs." Henry E. Luhrs was the founder's son-in-law and would succeed Martin Luther Beistle. There has been some

general confusion about this mark, with many collectors thinking Luhrs was a stand-alone company. Without exception, anything with the Luhrs mark is a Beistle product. From about 1948-1952, Beistle marked many items with their "Bee-Line" mark. This has a bee image in the center flanked by the words "Bee" and "Line" then encircled with the words "Made in U.S.A." Their manufactured items bear the actual "Bee-Line" mark only during this approximate four-year period. However, in catalogs and other marketing material Beistle continued to advertise their overall line of products as "Bee-Line" though the 1960s. Later markings through the early 1960s will have a copyright symbol present before the words "Beistle Co." As the 1960s drew to a close, "A Beistle Creation" in flowing script was the mark used. With all of this said, **many** Beistle items are not marked at all except with the words, "Made in USA."

The other prominent and imaginatively fertile paper ephemera manufacturer was Dennison. Dennison wasn't as diligent about varying its marks on products made over time, but it took pains to provide a mark on the vast majority of its output. Many of the products logically came in packaging clearly demarking Dennison as the manufacturer. The trick is to look for subtle differences in the packaging to provide an approximate date of production. Dennison's abundant variety of boxed gummed silhouettes, seals, party picks, place cards, etc. was marked with a now-obscure numbering system, when made in the teens through the mid 1920s. These boxes are generally monochromatic, except for the visible example of the specific product contained inside. As this decade progressed, these boxes lost their numbering but were otherwise unchanged. As the 1920s drew to a close, the fronts of these boxes were shaded a darker hue than the rest of the packaging. From this point on into the early 1930s, these shaded packages listed addresses on the reverse side. Only the last iteration of such packaging bore a London, England street address, even though Dennison had a presence in that city for several years beforehand. This awareness of the differences in packaging Dennison used should assist in the dating of their boxed, and some of their enveloped, products.

The Gibson Art Company of Cincinnati, Ohio, and the Whitney Company of Worcester, Massachusetts were two firms with very small output relative to Beistle and Dennison. Gibson is still in business today. Whitney, founded by George C.

Whitney in 1863 and primarily known today for valentines, closed in 1942. Decorative Halloween items from these firms are only sporadically marked and can be mainly identified through their art.

Manufacturers that catered primarily to the retail market sometimes used wholesalers to dispose of either unpopular goods or items that had been overproduced. There was a plethora of such wholesalers, and being able to peruse their catalogs can offer a wealth of information to those attempting to piece together the approximate manufacture date of treasured pieces. I say approximate because these wholesalers (B. Shackman and Company of New York City, Butler Brothers of St. Louis, H. Silberman and Sons of Milwaukee, and the Slack Manufacturing Company of Chicago among others) offered goods for sale sometimes for many years after the original manufacturer stopped producing the items.

A very precise way of dating an item is to actually find it pictured or referenced in catalogs that the savviest retail manufacturers regularly issued. Dennison was just such a manufacturer! Beginning in 1909 and continuing through 1934, these catalogs/decorating guides served as the primary sales and marketing tool

for Dennison's Halloween products. The 1909 Dennison Bogie Book is exceptionally rare with perhaps only a handful of copies extant. (Please see the Inner Sanctum section to see the example in this collection.) Dennison's uncertainty about whether this was a viable marketing tool perhaps is demonstrated by the fact that the second Bogie Book wasn't issued until 1912. World events intervened here and there, which prevented an unbroken string of annual issues, but by-and-large there is one for every year from 1912 through 1934. Later incarnations were sized and titled differently, but all followed the same general format. The Bogie Books through the early 1920s are a wealth of information as to what was being produced. After this time, although quite interesting, they tend to skew more toward generalities on decorating for parties, with hard data gleaned mainly through the profuse illustrations rather than a specific listing of available products. The actual Price List Pamphlets for years after about 1925 are where the real information is located. These are quite difficult to come by but relatively inexpensive when found. This type of paper ephemera was generally thrown away with nary a thought for the future collector. The original Bogie Books and their progeny help provide solid parameters for dating the Dennison product line.

As a fun aside, it's interesting to note the evolution of Dennison's sophistication in their approach to the Halloween parties market. Here is what is written on the first free page of their 1909 Bogie Book, on the cover of which appear two of what are described inside as "Dennison Bogie Chinamen":

According to Scotch superstition, Hallowe'en is the time when all the imps of earth and air hold annual carnival—witches, devils, goblins vie with skeletons in their shrouds in the mad celebration, and, attended by hideous and weird animals, mix and meddle in the affairs of mortals. A Hallowe'en Party affords, therefore, a wide field for fun and frolic.

Any hostess can easily select from this little book the scheme of decoration, the games and favors that will best entertain the guests she wishes to please. All the articles described are easily made. With Dennison's Crepe Paper and a little effort, any one can accomplish the results desired. If any difficulty arises, the paper experts at the various Dennison stores will be glad, by correspondence or personally, to explain and demonstrate.

As this excerpt demonstrates, the emphasis in 1909 was on the party-givers to buy the crepe paper and fashion for themselves the decorations illustrated inside. As the years rolled on, I believe Dennison realized they had a good thing going and aggressively sought to expand the boundaries of the holiday's decorations. In other words, they smartly created a need for their product offerings in the mind of the consumer rather than merely filling an already existing want. This pro-activity is certainly one of the reasons Dennison was so successful then and continues to be so in its present corporate incarnation today.

Let's examine a snippet from their 1917 Bogie Book, illustrating this evolution:

You are invited to send for patterns of any articles described in this book….The costumes, favors, Jack Horner Pies, etc. ARE *NOT* STOCK GOODS but can be quickly made from Dennison crepe paper and other materials.

On pages 32-36 STOCK GOODS are listed. These may be purchased of all local Dennison Dealers.

The following is from Dennison's 1923 Bogie Book:

The hostess who plans a Hallowe'en party has unlimited possibilities for both the character of her entertainment and fitting decorations. Black and orange are usually the predominating colors, while witches, black cats, bats, owls, bogies and Jack o'lanterns furnish a variety of appropriate decorative motifs.

Stock goods are listed in the price list at the back of the book. They may be purchased at stationers, department stores, many drug stores and at the five Dennison Stores.

By this time, Dennison was emphasizing their pre-packaged, or stock, goods, which undoubtedly carried a higher profit margin. They had also expanded the reach of their brand throughout the country by allowing a wide variety of retailers to carry their goods. Dennison—a clever company with clever goods!

Beistle, too, issued product catalogs but without the flair of their friendly competitor. These catalogs are quite difficult to locate, especially those from any point in the 1920s.

The final way to get a bead on dating your items is through an understanding of the evolution of the zip code system. The first step was city zoning. As the major metropolitan areas got larger, the Post Office began instituting simple city zones. If you see an address containing a number directly after the city, but before the state, you most assuredly have a piece dating no earlier than the later 1950s. Formal zip codes began to be required by the Post Office in July of 1963. Therefore any item containing a zip code was made after this time.

The key here is to understand all of this preceding data and try to put it into a coherent whole, so that when you examine an item you yourself can deduce its approximate age.

THE STATE OF THE MARKET

Values increased tremendously during the 1990s and continue to this day, albeit at a slower rate of increase. Values of the more common low-end items have moderated quite a bit, which is as it should be. As more collectors are exposed to what is routinely available in the market, the impetus to "get that item at all costs" abates tremendously. The acceptance and use of on-line auction venues has certainly contributed to this increase in the general sophistication of even the casual collector, as prospective bidders trolling through the electronic listings see many of the same items over and over again. Hopefully this book will also contribute to the collector's knowledge base.

As in any hobby, rising prices flush out long-held collections. This was especially true when one well-known collection was sold in two parts during 1997 through a gallery in Massachusetts. Another long-time collector cleverly pieced out his superb items via approximately seven auctions spaced out over several years. In the meantime, several lesser collections have also come onto the market, with all material quickly and, in many cases, expensively absorbed.

Unfortunately, the dark side to this overall rise in prices is the reproduced and fantasy items being brazenly hawked as vintage pieces—especially through the on-line venues. (A fantasy item is one that was never actually produced in the past but is being made now in a vintage style, often to fool collectors. A great example of a Halloween fantasy item is the nine inch, full-bodied, composition, horned red devil with a roll-out black paper tongue. Although nicely detailed and made in the old style, this item was produced in the 1990s and was among the first wave of such items to hit this country.) Novice collectors, the life blood of any continuing hobby, are unsuspectingly buying these often poorly made and soulless items, happily stuffing them into display cases unprepared for the disappointment due when, with further experience and knowledge, the realization hits that they have mistakenly purchased a non-vintage piece. I worry about the cynicism creeping into the vintage Halloween collecting hobby due to this avalanche of reproductions and fantasy items, which may drive off the newer collectors. That is one reason why this book should be useful and welcome. In these pages, I make available for inspection, quality vintage items to be used as a guide for those interested in this fun field.

There are a number of ways to differentiate vintage items from new items. These tips will be included in the verbiage at the beginning of most of the different sections where appropriate. One rule of thumb: Be very skeptical of anything hawked as being found in the former East Germany. Most, if not all, of these so-called vintage lanterns, horns, candy containers, nodders, and figurals have been recently made and are essentially decorative items only, with no vintage value. If you are buying Halloween items from dealers, get to know these people. Don't be hesitant to ask questions as to where they found items, how long they've had them in inventory, or how many similar items they've seen in the last few years. The most important question to ask of all, however, is how long do they stand behind all of the claims they make for their merchandise? Those dealers with the most sterling reputations will have the same answer—which is "forever." If you don't hear this magic word, and also see this magic word on your written receipt, I'd advise you to walk away—quickly.

I'd encourage all collectors to network. Through this activity, those dealers with the best and worst reputations will become known. If possible, see as many items in other collections as you can. It has been my experience that Halloween collectors are among the friendliest people on the planet! Get a good feel for what is out there. Knowledge is a wonderful and necessary commodity when you are a collector.

I believe the first grand phase of Halloween collecting has drawn to a close, and the overall market will see largely unchanging prices for a time. This is due to several factors, not the least of which are the soft economy and the suspicion that some items being offered for sale have been recently made. However, when the next cycle begins, I project that prices will escalate dramatically, and collectors will regret the items passed up in the interim between these cycles. I say this primarily because of what has already been pointed out—vintage display quality Halloween items are truly scarce. Because Halloween is an annual occasion creating new memories, this "renewable" aspect of the holiday will serve to keep interest in the old imagery strong in the coming years, attracting new collectors, all pursuing a dwindling supply of quality material.

About This Book

Every item in this book resides in my personal collection. Accompanying each photograph will be a caption containing information relative to each specific piece. First will be a simple descriptor like candy container or diecut, which will often include the material used to make the item. Following this will be the country of origin, when known; the specific manufacturer and where they operated, when known; the estimated year(s) of production with specific marks delineated where possible and necessary; the dimensions to the nearest one quarter inch; a "relative scarcity index" number; and the estimated value.

What is this relative scarcity index? It is a simple tool I have long used to separate scarcity and price in my mind. You won't find the precise relationship you'd expect between relative scarcity and price for every piece due to market quirks. Sometimes those items that are quite rare aren't valued as highly as you'd suspect. Alternatively, some very common items retain a surprisingly high value. It is a great tool with which to familiarize yourself. I use this 1 to 5 scale:

Relative Scarcity Index

(1) = Exceedingly rare and/or possibly unique

(2) = Rare

(3) = Scarce

(4) = Uncommon

(5) = Often Seen

The cited value of any item is for the condition shown and is my own estimate based on experience gained through attending antique shows and specialty auctions, visiting many shops throughout the United States, traipsing through the on-line world, and having countless conversations with collectors whom I have been fortunate to befriend. These valuations are not fixed and should be regarded as for reference only. Admittedly, the cited values of several of the stellar pieces may seem aggressive. However these values are either at or below offers which have been received privately, or they are at levels that would be fetched at a well-publicized and well-attended auction. Neither the author nor publisher is responsible for monetary losses that may occur to any person consulting this book for valuation information. Some say that values are obsolete from the moment a reference guide is published. I don't buy into that concept. The values cited here should provide a realistic baseline to use over time and can be adjusted up or down based on specific market conditions. These valuations, used in conjunction with the relative scarcity index, should arm even the most casual collector with useful data for the foreseeable future.

I truly enjoy hearing from other collectors. Whether you are just starting out or have been searching for these elusive items a long time, I'd love to hear your thoughts on this labor of love. My Web site is:

www.HalloweenCollector.com

Happy Halloween!

Mark B. Ledenbach

GAMES

A rich variety of Halloween-themed games are represented in this chapter. They tend to fall within these general categories: fortune, stunt, chance, and skill. Although all were designed to be played at parties, these vintage parties were primarily oriented to adults. Many of the fortune and stunt games were made for many seasons and are relatively common. The games of skill are harder to find, especially complete. A sub-category of these, the drawing games, are especially difficult to find as, like so many Halloween items, they were thrown away after a party ended. What I like about all of these examples is the diversity of imagery, the cleverness of the designs, and the basic sense of whimsy and fun they would bring to long-ago get-togethers.

Puzzle fortune game
USA, Beistle, (no mark)
1920s
5.75"H x 6"W, non-embossed
(3) **$30 each**
These are not often found intact because in
playing the game, you destroy it.

**Mystery Answer Board–
The Unconditional Oracle**
USA, Beistle, (diamond mark)
1925–1930
8.5"H x 5.75"W
(3) **$125**
Sample question:
Will my mate nag me?

**Witch's Mystery Answer Game–
The Unconditional Oracle**
USA, Beistle, (no mark)
1931–1935
12.5"H x 9.25"W
(4) **$75**
Sample question:
Will I live in a bungalow?

**Tongue Twister novelty game
with glassine envelope**
USA, The Gibson Art Company of
Cincinnati, Ohio
1928–1932
5.5"H x 6.75"W, non-embossed
(4) **$45**
Sample tongue twister: Sam Says
Sister Susie Thought She Saw Six
Slender Saplings.

Tongue Twister place cards
USA, The Gibson Art Company of
Cincinnati, Ohio
1928–1932
3.5"H x 4.25"W
non-embossed
(4) **$20 each**

◄ **Remember I've 9 Lives drawing game**
USA, The Gibson Art Company of
Cincinnati, Ohio
1930s
13.25"H x 21"W
(2) **$165**
Directions read: Give blindfolded guest a
good soft pencil–start him at "A" and see
him "finish" the cat.

◄ **Spook's Trip game**
USA, Beistle, (no mark)
1940s
6"H x 9"W
(4) **$55**

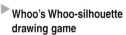

► **Whoo's Whoo-silhouette
drawing game**
USA, The Gibson Art Company
of Cincinnati, Ohio
1930s
25.75"H x 13"W
(2) **$165**

Feed the Kitty game
USA
1930s
8.5"H x 4.5"W
(3) $95

Hallowe'en Party game
USA, Saalfield Publishing Company of Akron, Ohio
copyrighted 1907
28"H x 18"W
(3) $125
There is a stock number of 702 in the lower left corner.

Hallowe'en Party Game in envelope
USA, Saalfield Publishing Company of Akron, Ohio
1910–1919
Envelope: 11.5"H x 8.25"W
Board: 24"H x 18"W
(3) $60

Hitchy Witchy game
USA, Beistle
(HE Luhrs mark)
1940s
5.25"H x 9.5"W
(3) $80
This skill game has dual-sided lithography.

Pumpkin Face Ring Game
USA, Schacht Rubber
Manufacturing Company of
Huntington, Indiana
copyrighted 1927
9.25"H x 7"W
(2) **$275**

**Spook Kat Luminous
Party Game**
USA, American Novelty
Company of Omaha,
Nebraska
1930s
Envelope: 11"H x 8.5"W
Board: 19"H x 19.25"W
(3) **$65**

**Owl Tell Your Fortune
game**
USA, Beistle, (no mark)
1940s
9.25"H x 6"W
(4) **$40**

Ring the "Belle" toss game
USA, (probably the Gibson Art Company)
1930s
Cone: 16"H x 8"W, Rings: 7" diameter
(1) **$450**
Printed on one ring is: Here's Your
Chance! Do It Right Off The Bat!
Printed on the two others is: Your
Some "Punkins" If You Ring The
"Belle." ("Your" should be "You're"
but the manufacturer is entitled to an
error now and again!)

▲ **Kitty Card Game**
USA, Beistle, (stated on instructions)
copyrighted 1927
5.5"H x 4.75"W
(3) **$125**
This game, designed for four players, consists of
directions and 30 illustrated cards.

▲ **Hallowe'en Witch Spot Game**
USA, Beistle, (stated on instructions)
copyrighted 1930
7.25"H x 5.75"W
(3) **$120**
This is a seasonally themed bingo game.

▲ **WITCH-EE The Animated Fortune Teller game**
USA, Selchow & Righter Company of New York, New York
1925–1930
6.5" square
(3) **$200**
This comes with fortune cards and a chamois.

▲ **Jack-O-Lantern Target game**
USA, Parker Brothers, Inc. of Salem, Massachusetts
1929–1932
5.5"H x 13.75"W
(2) **$750**
This complete game consists of a toy rifle, nine cork bullets, four connected
targets resting on wooden stabilizing blocks, and an advertising card. It was
assigned a stock number of 455. The rifle is rarely found with the game, and
it contributes significantly to the value.

GAMES

Stunt Hallowe'en Quiz
USA, Beistle, (HE Luhrs mark)
1940s
9"H x 8.75"W
(5) **$35**
Sample question: Do I look young? Sample answer:
Yodel. If it sounds terrible the answer is yes.

Old Witch Brewsome Stunts
USA, Beistle, (no mark, but it appeared in their 1948
catalog as a newly released item)
1948–1950s
9.25"H x 7.5"W
(4) **$45**

Jack-O-Lantern Game
USA
1950s
6"H x 9"W
(4) **$30**

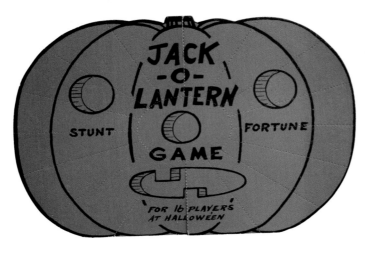

Left: **Ghostly Stunt and Fortune Game**
USA, Beistle, (no mark)
1940s
4"H x 6"W
(5) **$30**

Right: **Zingo Halloween Fortune
and Stunt Game**
USA, Beistle, (printed on item)
copyrighted 1935
11.5"H x 8.25"W
(5) **$35**
It has unusual scalloped edges.
Sample stunt: Whistle Yankee Doodle
with a saucepan on your noodle.

Hoo's Next Game of Stunts
USA, Beistle, (HE Luhrs mark)
copyrighted 1940
8"H x 8.75"W
(4) **$50**

Children's Take A Chance Stunt Game
USA
1930s
8.25"H x 8.75"W
(4) **$55**

Left: **Fortune Telling Favor Set**
USA, (probably Beistle)
1940s
4"H x 3.25"W
(4) **$30**
It comes with 10 favors and a direction sheet.

Right: **Hallowe'en Fortunes**
USA, Beistle, (no mark)
1940s
8"H x 6.5"W
(4) **$65**
The pairing of these items shows how manufacturers would use essentially the same artwork for different kinds of products, heightening production efficiencies.

I'm a Dumbskull Stunt Game
USA, Beistle, (diamond mark)
1925–1930
Game: 12.5"H x 9.25"W, Envelope: 13"H x 10"W
(4) **$65**
There are two board variations. The less common version has a parrot on top, a clock dial at the base with a metal spinner, and no easel. The envelope shown is for this version. The other version (shown) has a cat on top, no clock dial or metal spinner, and an easel.

Crystal Fortunes game
USA, Beistle
(HE Luhrs mark)
copyrighted 1940
12"H x 4.5"W
(5) **$35**

Fortunes By the Luminous Spirit (board with fortunes card)
USA, American Novelty Company of Omaha, Nebraska
1930s
Board: 14"H x 11"W, Card: 14"H x 4"W
(3) **$95**

Fortune Wheel for Hallowe'en Parties
USA, Beistle, (no mark)
1928–1931
11.25"H x 8.25"W
(3) **$125**
It has a honeycomb base with two fold-out flaps containing fortunes.

Halloween Pie fortune games
USA, Beistle, (Bee-Line mark)
1948–1952
6" diameter
(4) **$35 each**
There are 10 wedges for each pie and three pies in the complete series.

Fortune Wheel for Hallowe'en Parties
USA, Beistle, (no mark)
1931–1935
12.5"H x 9.25"W
(3) **$85**
It has an easel attached to the back.

▲ **Spin-O-Rama Halloween Stunt and Fortune Game**
USA, Beistle, (A Beistle Creation mark)
1960s
18.25"H x 12.25"W
(5) **$20**

◄ **Cat and Witch Party Game**
USA, Whitman Publishing Company of Racine, Wisconsin
1940s
Box: 10.25"H x 7.75"W
Board: 19"H x 21"W
(5) **$35**
A stock number of 3016 is on the box.

◄ **Jack-O-Lantern Fortune Game**
USA, Beistle, (diamond mark)
1925–1930
12.5"H x 9.5"W
(3) **$150**
It has a fold-out prop base and a patent number of 1616568.

GAMES

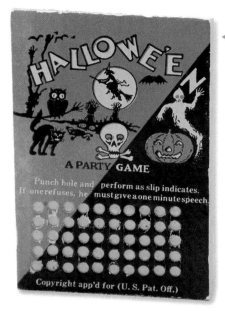

Hallowe'en: A Party Game punchboard
USA
1950s
3.75"H x 2.5"W
(5) **$15**

Hallowe'en Pumpkin Fortune Game
USA, Beistle, (diamond mark)
1925–1930
7"H x 5.5"W
(2) **$250**
There are two packaging variations: a boxed game and a game in an envelope. These are otherwise identical and are valued equally. A stock number of 874 is in the lower right corner of this example.

Hallowe'en Wheel Witch Fortune Game
USA, Beistle, (no mark)
copyrighted 1936
Game: 9"H x 5.5"W, Card: 10"H x 5.75"W
(2) **$350**
This item has a rarely incorporated "mechanical" action feature. This is complete with original glassine envelope and the often-missing fortune card.

Package of "16 Stunts for a Hallowe'en Party"
USA, Beistle, (no mark)
1930s
4"H x 5.25"W
(3) **$65**
A stock number of 629 is in the lower right corner.

Ringer Hallowe'en Donut Toss Stunt Game
USA, Beistle, (printed on box)
copyrighted 1935
6.5"H x 7.75"W
(3) **$100**
The cat diecut is lightly embossed.

Hallowe'en Stunt Game
USA, Beistle, (diamond mark)
1925–1930
7.25"H x 5.75"W
(2) **$250**
A stock number of 376 is in the lower right corner.

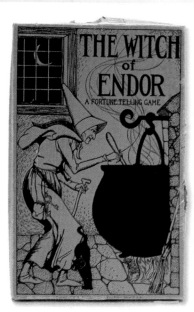

◀ The printed interior of the box lid to The Witch of Endor.

▲ **The Witch of Endor: A Fortune Telling Game**
USA, Maumkegg Game Company of Salem, Massachusetts
copyrighted 1929
10.5"H x 6.5"W
(3) **$75**

25

Lanterns and Shades

Some of the earliest Halloween items fall into this category, beginning with the tin parade lanterns manufactured in the United States (primarily Toledo, Ohio) in the first decade of the twentieth century. Tabletop variations of these were made as well. These metal lanterns quickly gave way to pressed paper items made in Germany then to the plethora of pulp lanterns manufactured in the United States. Earlier lanterns would typically have a holder for a candle, but as the danger inherent in such designs became apparent, candleholders gradually disappeared. Shades, mainly designed to hang over light bulbs, also became a staple of decorating.

Reproductions of lanterns have become abundant, and collectors need to be careful. The original pulp lanterns made in the United States decades ago will have one or two indented molded rings on the bottom. Although not a sure sign of authenticity, it is a feature to look for when considering one for purchase, as most of the reproductions have flat bottoms. The paper inserts for lanterns have been reproduced to such an extent that collectors should always assume they are not vintage, and should be hesitant to pay any premium for supposed vintage inserts.

Metal parade lantern
USA
1905–1910
7" in diameter
(3) **$900**
It opens at the center and is designed for an interior candle.
The paper insert is almost always missing, having been burned
away. This example has the original internal hardware and
wooden finial.

**Pulp black cat face on fence
lantern with original insert**
USA
1940–1950s
7.5"H x 6.25"W
(5) **$150**
This item was made for many
seasons and is quite common.
REPRO ALERT: This item has
been widely reproduced.
Originals will have an indented
circle at the bottom, whereas
most, if not all, of the
reproductions will have a flat
bottom. Also, quite a cottage
industry has arisen in the
reproduction of paper inserts. A
safe assumption is that all
inserts are reproductions.

Left: **Shade with alternating
JOLs and cat faces, all with
differing expressions**
USA
1930s
3.75"H x 5"W
(3) **$65**
Right: **Black cat face shade
with unusual white backing**
Germany
1920s
2.75"H x 5"W
(2) **$75**

◄ **Shade with alternating JOLs and cat faces all with differing expressions**
USA
1930s
3.25"H x 4.5"W
(4) **$45**

▶ **Dual-sided cardboard black cat face lantern with slot and tab construction**
USA
1940s
6.5"H x 2.5"W x 6"L
(4) **$165**
This was manufactured without inserts.

▲ **Dual-sided cardboard black cat face lantern with slot and tab construction and original inserts**
USA
1950s
7.5"H x 3.25"W x 6.5"L
(5) **$65**
The other side shows a smiling cat face.

▶ **Dual-sided black cat face lantern with differing expressions**
USA
1930s
7.5"H x 9"L
(3) **$115**

Four-sided black cat lantern
USA
1930s
8"H x 5.25"W
(2) **$135**

**Cardboard lantern
with entirely differing
sides**
USA
pre-1920s
7.25"H x 3.25"W x 8.25"L
(2) **$225**
It was a surprise seeing this in a
1917 dry goods catalog, as the
vintage was always assumed to be
1950s, based on the design and
construction. This was
manufactured without inserts.

**Black cat transparency behind which
a candle would be placed on the
attached holder**
USA, Beistle, (HE Luhrs mark)
1940s
8.5"H x 6"W
(2) **$175**
Later iterations have the Beistle "Bee-
Line" mark and have a lesser value. This is
one of a set of four similarly sized. The
others are an owl, witch, and a JOL, with
the JOL being the rarest.

**Pulp black cat face lantern with original
insert**
USA
1940–1950s
5.25"H x 7"W
(4) **$200**
This item was made for many seasons in both
orange and black.
REPRO ALERT: This item has been widely
reproduced. Originals will have an indented circle
at the bottom, whereas most, if not all, of the
reproductions will have a flat bottom. Also, quite a
cottage industry has arisen in the reproduction of
paper inserts. A safe assumption is that all inserts
are reproductions.

▶ **Identical dual-sided heavy cardboard black cat face lantern with slot and tab construction and original inserts**
USA
1950s
7.5"H x 3"W x 6"L
(5) **$75**

▲ **Identical dual-sided black cat face lantern**
USA, Beistle, (no mark)
1940s
8.75"H x 12.5"L
(4) **$145**

▲ **Four-sided skull & crossbones lantern**
USA
late 1940s–1950s
10"H x 5"W
(5) **$45**
This was made for many seasons and is plentiful. About 150 new old stock of these lanterns were discovered in the late 1990s, which depressed their value considerably.

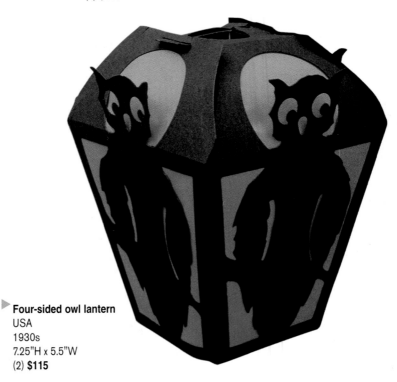

▶ **Four-sided owl lantern**
USA
1930s
7.25"H x 5.5"W
(2) **$115**

Six-sided owl shade
USA
1920s
10.5"H x 12"W
(3) **$115**
It has an interior cardboard crossbar into which a light bulb can be inserted. The brace is marked "Made in U.S. AM."

Owl transparency behind which a candle would be placed on the attached holder
USA, Beistle, (HE Luhrs mark)
copyrighted 1940
8.5"H x 6"W
(2) **$175**
Later iterations have the Beistle "Bee-Line" mark and have a lesser value. This is one of a set of four similarly sized. The others are a cat, witch, and a JOL, with the JOL being the rarest.

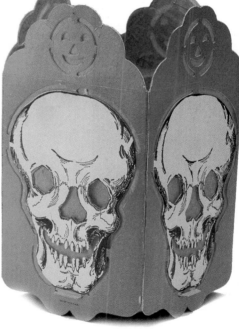

Four-sided skull lantern
USA, (probably Beistle)
1920–1930s
10.5"H x 5.5"W
(3) **$100**

Identical dual-sided owl face lantern
USA, Beistle, (no mark)
1940s
9.5"H x 12"L
(4) **$55**

◀ **Two examples of four-sided lanterns with each panel differing in imagery**
USA, (probably Beistle)
1920–1930s
6.5"H x 3.5"W
(4) **$75 each**

▶ **Two examples of four-sided lanterns with each panel differing in imagery**
USA, (probably Beistle)
1920–1930s
Left: 9.5"H x 4.75"W
(3) **$125**
Right: 10"H x 5.5"W
(3) **$135**

▼ **Four-sided shade with differing imagery on each panel**
USA
1930s
4.25"H x 4.5"W
(2) **$95**

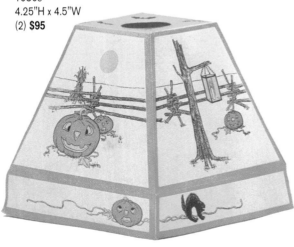

▲ **Four-sided shade with differing imagery on each panel**
USA
1930s
3.5"H x 4.25"W
(2) **$125**
A Halloween teepee is highly unusual imagery.

LANTERNS AND SHADES

32

Four-sided Spos'N lantern with each panel having differing imagery and text
USA
1920s
10.75"H x 6"W
(2) **$225**
The earliest versions, like this example, have cutout silhouettes as part of the main frame, rather than having these images printed directly onto the orange area. These early versions are more rare, and they have a value significantly greater than later versions.

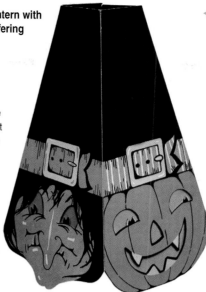

Four-sided shade with alternating images of JOLs and witch faces, each with differing expressions
USA, The Gibson Art Company of Cinicinnati, Ohio
(Note its similarity to the "Ring the Belle" game)
late 1940s
11.5"H x 6"W
(2) **$175**

Left: **Pulp devil head lantern with original insert**
USA
1930s
5.5"H x 6.75"W
(3) **$400**
Right: **Pulp devil head lantern with original insert**
USA, F.N. Burt Company of Buffalo, New York
1930s
(3) **$450**
This item appears in a Butler Brothers catalog from 1932. Earlier versions, like this example, were spray painted from below giving the lantern a cleverly faux-lit look.

Left: **Heavy cardboard dual-sided skull lantern with original inserts and slot and tab construction**
USA
1940s
7.25"H x 3"W x 6"L
(4) **$95**
REPRO ALERT: This lantern has been reproduced. Authentic items will have a tan patina, whereas the reproductions are stark white.
Right: **Heavy cardboard dual-sided devil face lantern with original inserts and slot and tab construction**
USA
1940s
7.5"H x 3"W x 6.5"L
(5) **$75**
REPRO ALERT: This lantern has been reproduced using a thinner and glossier cardboard stock than the originals.

▲ **Four-sided shade that would hang down over a light bulb**
USA, (probably Beistle)
1930s
9.25"H x 6.25"W
(2) **$200**
Each panel has differing imagery.

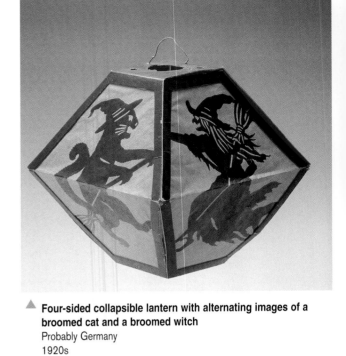

▲ **Four-sided collapsible lantern with alternating images of a broomed cat and a broomed witch**
Probably Germany
1920s
7"H x 6.5"W
(2) **$150**
Interestingly, the cat's head is identical to the image on one of the versions of Beistle's "I'm A Dumbskull" game. This could be another instance of an association between Beistle and German artisans.

▼ **Four-sided collapsible lantern with imagery identical to the shade shown above**
USA, (probably Beistle)
1930s
8.25"H x 6.5"W
(2) **$175**

▼ **Four-sided shade with a decorative bottom and differing imagery on each panel**
USA
1930s
7.5"H x 4.5"W
(2) **$150**

Two-sided lantern with unusual blue coloration
USA
1920s
10.25"H x 9"W
(3) **$125**
The somewhat oval bottom piece for the candle is often missing, although not with this example.

Large JOL head transparency behind which a candle would be placed on the attached holder
USA, Beistle, (HE Luhrs mark)
1940s
14"H x 8.5"W
(2) **$185**
Later iterations have the Beistle "Bee-Line" mark and have a lesser value. This is one of a set of three similarly sized. The others are a cat and a witch, with the cat being the rarest.

▲ **Two-sided lantern with JOLs of differing expressions**
USA
1920s
6.5"H x 5.5"W
(2) **$125**

▲ **Cat's face shade**
USA
Dennison
1930s
7.25" diameter
(2) **$65**

▶ **Cardboard six panel
shade with printed
paper inserts**
Germany
1920s
5.25"H x 6.25"W
(4) **$75**
It is heavily embossed.

◀ **Four-sided shade with differing imagery on each panel**
USA
1930s
4"H x 5"W
(2) **$80**

▶ **Four-sided shade with alternating identical images**
USA
1930s
5"H x 4.5"W
(2) **$100**

◀ **Dual-sided slot and tab JOL lantern with differing expressions and original inserts**
USA, The Dolly Toy Company of Tipp City, Ohio
1950s
6.5"H x 3.5"W x 8"L
(5) **$60**

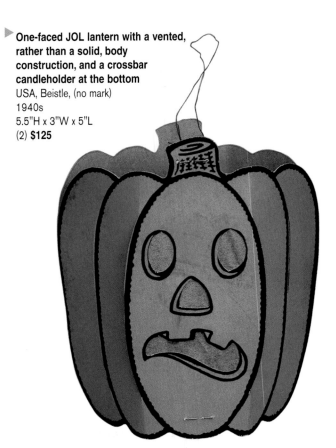

One-faced JOL lantern with a vented, rather than a solid, body construction, and a crossbar candleholder at the bottom
USA, Beistle, (no mark)
1940s
5.5"H x 3"W x 5"L
(2) **$125**

Large witch-head transparency behind which a candle would be placed on the attached holder
USA, Beistle, (HE Luhrs mark)
1940s
14"H x 8.5"W
(2) **$235**
Later iterations have the Beistle "Bee-Line" mark and have a lesser value. This is one of a set of three similarly sized. The others are a cat and a JOL-head, with the cat being the rarest.

Trio of dual-sided JOL slot and tab lanterns with original inserts
USA
1950s
Left: 4.5"H x 3.25"W x 5.25"L (4), **$50**
Middle: 5"H x 3.75"W x 6.5"L (5), **$50**
Right: 6.25"H x 4.5"W x 8"L (5), **$50**

Dual-sided JOL lantern with differing expressions
USA, Beistle, (no mark)
1930s
5"H x 2.5"W x 8"L
(2) **$150**

Dual-sided JOL lantern with differing expressions and a vented, rather than a solid, body construction, and a crossbar candleholder at the bottom
USA, Beistle, (no mark)
1940s
12.5"H x 8.75"W x 14.5"L
(1) **$250**
This huge lantern was probably for a store display, accounting for its great rarity.

One-faced JOL lantern with a vented, rather than a solid, body construction and a crossbar candleholder at the bottom
USA, Beistle, (no mark)
1940s
6.5"H x 4.25"W x 7.5"L
(2) **$115**

Identical dual-sided JOL lantern with slot and tab top and bottom supports and honeycomb sides
USA, Beistle, (no mark)
1938
11.25"H x 4"W x 12"L
(2) **$225**
Beistle also made this lantern in a slightly smaller size.

39

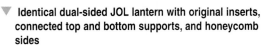

▲ **Identical dual-sided JOL lantern with yellow cardboard sides connected to the main faces with metal clips**
USA, Beistle, (no mark)
1938
11.5"H x 4.75"W x 12.5"L
(2) **$150**

▼ **Identical dual-sided JOL lantern with original inserts, connected top and bottom supports, and honeycomb sides**
USA, Beistle, (printed name)
1930–1931
11"H x 3.75"W x 12"L
(2) **$800**
This stunning, and much sought-after lantern, represents the high-water mark of Beistle artistry in its sophistication and imaginative rendering. It was also made in an 8" size. Both are quite rare, especially when intact.

▼ **Dual-sided JOL lantern with original inserts, top and bottom supports and orange tissue (not honeycomb) sides**
Made in Germany for Beistle
1928
11.25"H x 3.5"W x 12.25"L
(2) **$475**
This lantern tells a great story. It is an example of the short-lived formal association Beistle had in the late 1920s with German artists and producers, hence the "Made in Germany" mark. It also shows the evolution from this curiously flat German design to the robustness of the memorable Beistle-USA lantern from 1930–1931.

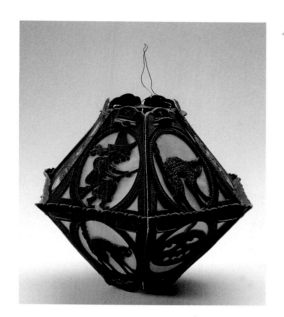

Cardboard 12-panel collapsible lantern with orange paper backing
Germany
1920s
7"H x 10.5"W
(2) **$300**
It is heavily embossed.

Ribbed collapsible JOL-faced lantern with a wooden top and bottom
Japan
1920s
16"H x 13.75"W
(1) **$275**

Fold-up JOL-faced lantern with differing faces on each side
Germany
1920s
16" diameter
(3) **$90**
REPRO ALERT: This lantern has been reproduced with many iterations of imagery beginning in the 1990s. Although it is difficult to discern new from old, new lanterns will have thinner paper stock, brighter colors, more sophisticated designs, and a flimsy gauge metal folding frame.

Collapsible lantern with two differing faces
Japan
1920s
4.5"H x 4"W
(2) **$140**

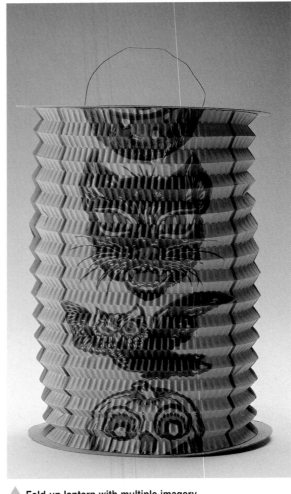

▲ **Ornately designed 12-panel collapsible lantern**
Made in Germany for Beistle
1928
7"H x 9"W
(5) **$115**
This lantern was produced in great quantities and was wholesaled for several years after production. About 150 old stock of this lantern was discovered in the mid-1990s, greatly reducing their value.

▲ **Fold-up lantern with multiple imagery**
Germany
1920s
12"H x 9"W
(3) **$60**

▶ **Cardboard six-panel shade with printed paper inserts**
Germany
1920s
5.25"H x 6.25"W
(4) **$65**
It is heavily embossed.

◄ **Four-sided shades**
Germany (probably made
for Beistle)
1920s
4.75"H x 6"W
Left: (4) **$90**
Right: (3) **$90**

◄ **Four-sided owl face shade**
Germany (probably made for
Beistle)
1920s
4.75"H x 6"W
(3) **$65**

▶ **Round shade with unusual factory-
made pinholes surrounding the main
designs to emit light more easily**
Germany
1930s
4"H x 6.25"W
(2) **$175**
There are six faces along the rim, each
with a differing expression.

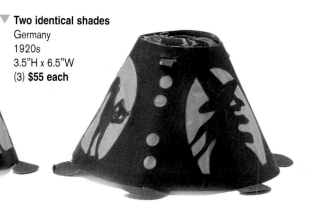

▼ **Two identical shades**
Germany
1920s
3.5"H x 6.5"W
(3) **$55 each**

43

▲ **Identical two-sided JOL lantern**
Germany
1930s
3.5"H x 2.25"W x 3.5"L
(3) **$215**

▼ **Cardboard four-panel shade with orange paper backing**
Germany
1920s
8.5"H x 5.5"W
(2) **$325**
It is heavily embossed.

▼ **Cardboard four-panel lantern with latched door**
Germany 1920s
9"H x 5.5"W
(2) **$550**
It is heavily embossed.
REPRO ALERT: This lantern was reproduced beginning in the early 1990s. Although the dimensions and artwork are identical, the black cardboard is quite thin and somewhat glossy on the reproductions. Also, the orange paper backing is overly bright on the reproductions.

Molded cardboard ghost head lantern with original red crepe insert
Germany
1920s
5"H x 6.5"W
(2) **$800**

Composition devil head lantern with original inserts and crepe collar
Germany
1920s
3.75"H
(2) **$800**

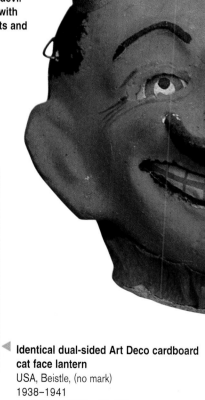

Identical dual-sided Art Deco cardboard cat face lantern
USA, Beistle, (no mark)
1938–1941
11.25"H x 3.5"W x 11.25"L
(3) **$225**
There are two iterations: one with orange honeycomb sides and one without. Both are valued equally. Beistle marketed these as "Tommy Whiskers" lanterns.

CANDY CONTAINERS, NODDERS, AND FIGURALS

Many of the German items in this chapter were made in "cottage industries," miniscule manufacturing operations wherein the items emerging from the molds would be hand assembled and then hand decorated. The workers were free to add their own touches to the pieces, which accounts for the variation in items seen today made from the same molds. German candy containers, nodders, and figurals were made in very small quantities. Few, in absolute terms, have survived in decent condition, which accounts for their high values. The earliest German items were made from a heavy composition. The composition used became lighter, and perhaps more finely made, as time progressed. What is composition? There is not a single answer, but one answer is this: Composition is an amalgamation of gypsum, sawdust, glues, other paper-based fibers, and other materials that were liquefied and then poured into molds to harden. Fragile overall, it is a material that accepts a variety of paints well, and is easily molded into many different shapes. Once purchased, the new owner would fill candy containers with hard candies. Candies like the hard cinnamon hearts still available today could have been used, as could any other non-sticky confection.

Reproductions and fantasy pieces are a major problem for German items. These have gotten so pervasive that I will not buy a German candy container, nodder, or figural unless I can personally inspect it, or I am buying from a dealer whom I trust.

It is difficult to tell with absolute certainty whether a composition piece was made seventy years ago or seven days ago. One unscientific method I use is to pick up the piece, hold it tightly, and feel if it is colder than the surrounding air. Many of the materials from which new items are made today don't retain ambient heat well, so they are almost always cold to the touch. Another simple test is to pick up and smell an item. New pieces retain an easily detected paint odor for up to 18 months after production. Other ways to detect whether a piece is vintage come from experience: being familiar enough with the types of interior papers used; the state of the composition; the care taken with the painted details; the hues of the paints themselves; the inks used in the marks, etc.

This chapter also contains pieces not made in Germany. Any reproduction issues with these items have been delineated in the individual captions.

Left: **JOL candy box**
USA
1950s
4.75" diameter
(4) **$30**
It is lightly embossed.

Right: **JOL dual-sided candy box**
USA, Ann-Dee Specialties of Bayside, New York
1950s
4.25"H x 3.75"W
(4) **$30**

Dual-sided broomed witch candy container
USA, Ann-Dee Specialties of Bayside, New York
1950s
8"H x 2"W x 8"L
(3) **$50**

JOL heavy cardboard candy box
USA
1950s
7.5"H x 7.5"W
(4) **$35**

Left: **Halloween Pumpkin candy purse**
USA, E. Rosen Company of Providence, Rhode Island
1950s
4.25"H x 5.5"W
(4) **$40**

Right: **Candy box**
USA
1958–1960
5.25"H x 3"W
(3) **$40**

◄ **Pair of slot and tab dual-sided candy containers**
USA
1950s
Left: **Witch pulling JOL**
4.5"H x 2.5"W x 8"L
(3) **$95**
Right: **Cat pulling pumpkin house**
4.5"H x 2.5"W x 7.75"L
(3) **$95**
The wheels turn on both.

► *Left:* **JOL candy box**
USA, Candy Crafters, Inc. of Lansdowne, Pennsylvania
1950s
4.25"H x 5.5"W
(3) **$45**
Right: **JOL man dual-sided candy cup**
USA, Beistle, (no mark)
1960–1962
5"H x 4"W
(3) **$30**

◄ **Scarecrow couple slot and tab dual-sided candy container**
USA
1950s
4.25"H x 2.75"W x 5.5"L
(3) **$70**

► **Broomed witch by chimney dual-sided candy container**
probably USA, no mark
1950s
6"H x 3.25"W x 7.5"L
(4) **$65**
It is made from heavy cardboard.

◀ **Trio of slot and tab dual-sided candy containers**
USA, G.M. Company
1950s
Left: **Skeleton pulling wagon**
marked HR5-A
3.75"H x 2"W x 5.25"L
(3) **$70**
Middle: **Cat in JOL car**
marked HR5-D
4.25"H x 2"W x 4.5"L
(4) **$60**
Right: **Witch at cauldron**
marked HR5-F
4"H x 2"W x 4"L
(3) **$65**

▼ **Cat driving a JOL car candy container**
USA, G.M. Company
1950s, marked RH-6C
7.5"H x 3"W x 10.75"L
(2) **$125**
It is made from heavy cardboard.

▼ **Black cat face candy box**
USA, Candy Crafters, Inc. of Lansdowne, Pennsylvania
1950s
4.25"H x 4.75"W
(3) **$50**

▼ **Trio of slot and tab dual-sided candy containers**
USA, G.M. Company
1950s
Left: **Witch in shoe car,** marked HR5-E, 3.75"H x 2.25"W x 4.25"L, (3) **$75**
Middle: **Broomed witch,** marked HR5-B, 3.5"H x 2"W x 4.5"L, (3) **$75**
Right: **Pirate ship,** marked HR5-C, 4.5"H x 2.25"W x 5.5"L, (4) **$30**

49

▼ **Black cat pulling JOL slot and tab candy container**
USA, A Fibro Toy manufactured by the Dolly Toy Company of Dayton, Ohio
1946–1949
5.5"H x 3.25"W x 8.5"L
(3) **$165**
It is made from heavy cardboard and has wood wheels. Later iterations have no markings on the underside. These are more common and have a lesser value.
REPRO ALERT: Reproductions from the 1990s are made from a thinner, high gloss paper stock.

► **JOL-headed man pulling cart slot and tab candy container**
USA, A Fibro Toy manufactured by the Dolly Toy Company of Dayton, Ohio
1946–1949
6.5"H x 3.25"W x 7"L
(2) **$200**
It is made from heavy cardboard and has wood wheels. Later iterations have no markings on the underside. These are more common and have a lesser value.

▲ **Witch pulling hay wagon slot and tab candy container**
USA, A Fibro Toy manufactured by the Dolly Toy Company of Dayton, Ohio
1946–1949
6.75"H x 2.75"W x 9.5"L
(3) **$165**
It is made from heavy cardboard and has wood wheels. Later iterations have no markings on the underside. These are more common and have a lesser value.
REPRO ALERT: Reproductions from the 1990s are made from a thinner, high gloss paper stock.

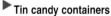
► **Tin candy containers**
USA, Tindeco
1930s
Left: 1.75"H x 4"W
(5) **$60**
The base is decorated with owls, bats, witches, and cats.
Right: 1.75"H x 6"W
(5) **$80**
The lid's rim is decorated with a fruit motif.

◀ **Trio of tin litho JOL candy containers**
USA, US Metal Toy Mfg. Company
1950s
Left: 5.25"H x 6.5"W
(4) **$80**
Plastic horn nose.
Middle: 4"H x 5"W
(5) **$45**
Right: 4.75"H x 6.5"W
(5) **$70**
Plastic horn nose.

◀ **Reverse sides of the items above.**

▶ **Trio of composition
Veggie figurals**
Germany
early 1930s
2.5"H
(3) **$115 each**

◀ **Trio of composition
Veggie figurals**
Germany
1920s
Left: 4"H
(3) **$165**
Middle: 3.75"H
(3) **$165**
Right: 3.25"H
(3) **$165**

◀ *Left:* **Composition Veggie woman candy container (opens at bottom)**
Germany
1920s
4.75"H
(3) **$200**
Right: **Composition Veggie woman figural**
Germany
1920s
4.5"H
(2) **$200**

▲ **Two composition Veggie children candy containers (both open at neck)**
Germany
pre-1920s
Left: 2.5"H
(3) **$265**
Right: 2.75"H
(4) **$150**

▲ **Two composition Veggie man boxing figurals**
Germany
1920s
4.25"H
(2) **$185 each**

▶ **Trio of composition Veggie figurals**
Germany
1920s
Left: 3.75"H
(3) **$165**
Middle: 4"H
(2) **$195**
Right: 4"H
(3) **$165**

◀ **An elusive composition Veggie musical band**
Germany
1920s
Left: 4.25"H
Figural
(3) **$175**
Middle Left: 4"H
Figural
(2) **$225**
Middle Right: 4"H
Candy container (opens at neck)
(2) **$325**
Right: 4"H
Figural
(3) **$175**

◀ **Heavy composition Veggie boy candy container (opens at neck)**
Germany
pre-1920s
4.75"H
(1) **$525**

▲ **Heavy composition Veggie pirate candy container (opens at neck)**
Germany
pre-1920s
4.25"H
(2) **$500**

◀ **Two composition Veggie military officer (astride fruit) candy containers (bottom plugs)**
Germany
pre-1920s
Left: 3.25"H
(1) **$650**
Right: 3"H
(1) **$650**

◄ **JOL-faced drum candy container (opens at bottom) with a trio of repeated images of Veggie kids circling the middle**
Germany
1920s
2.75"H x 2"W
(1) **$825**
It is lithoed paper over cardboard.

▼ **JOL-faced hat box candy container (top lid removes)**
Germany
1920s
1.75"H x 1.75"W
Below: **Top view of JOL-faced hat box candy container**
(2) **$300**
It is made of lithoed paper over light cardboard, string, and one metal clasp.
Two stickers are on the side: Express! and 36.

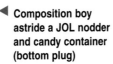

◄ **Composition boy astride a JOL nodder and candy container (bottom plug)**
Germany
early 1930s
2.75"H
(2) **$325**
The head is on a flexible metal strip.

► *Left:* **JOL-faced purse candy container (opens at center)**
Germany
1920s
1.75"H x 1.5"W x 2.75"L
(3) **$325**
It is lithoed paper over cardboard, string.

◀ **Composition Veggie creature candy container (opens at neck) with wooden base**
Germany
1920s
5"H
(3) **$350**

◀ **Heavy composition Veggie creature candy container (bottom plug)**
Germany
pre-1920s
4.75"H
(2) **$375**

◀ *Left:* **JOL-faced four-sided railroad lantern candy container (opens at bottom)**
Germany
1920s
4.5"H x 2.5"W
(1) **$875**
It is lithoed paper over cardboard.
Right: **JOL-faced drum candy container (opening at bottom held in place by wood stick)**
Germany
1920s
Drum: 2.75"H x 2.5"W
Drumstick: 4.75"L
(1) **$900**
It is made of lithoed paper over cardboard with a wooden drumstick.

◀ **Watermelon candy container (opens at center)**
Austria
1920s
2.5"H x 2.5"W x 4"L
(4) **$200**
It is lithoed paper over cardboard.

◄ **Skull with top hat candy container (bottom plug)**
Germany
1920s
3"H
(1) **$500**
It is made of lithoed paper over cardboard with a molded cardboard top hat.

◄ **Composition JOL-head candy container (bottom plug)**
Germany
1920s
3.25"H
(2) **$500**

◄ **Composition JOL-head with top hat candy container (bottom plug)**
Germany
1920s
3.75"H
(2) **$550**
The flaking of the black is characteristic of the paint used when made. Most pieces today with this paint will exhibit signs of flaking.

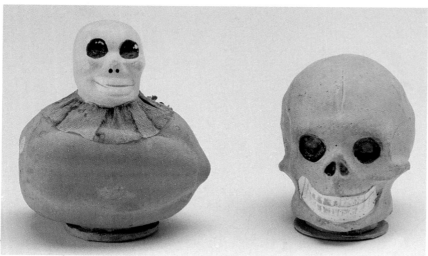

◄ *Left:* **Composition skull with crepe collar emerging from pumpkin candy container (bottom plug)**
Germany
1920s
3"H x 2.25"W x 2.75"L
(2) **$475**
Right: **Composition skull candy container (bottom plug)**
Germany
pre-1920s
2.5"H
(3) **$350**

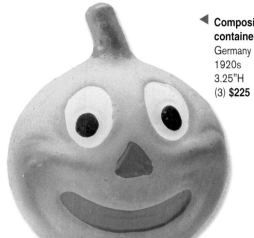

◀ **Composition JOL candy container (bottom plug)**
Germany
1920s
3.25"H
(3) **$225**

◀ **JOL candy container with movable reticulated hat (opens at center)**
Germany
pre-1920s
5.75"H x 3.5"W
(2) **$600**
It is made of molded cardboard, fringed paper, and wood.

◀ **Watermelon candy container (opens at bottom)**
Germany
1920s
4"H
(2) **$425**

◀ *Left:* **Composition Grim Reaper candy container (opens at bottom)**
Germany
1920s
3.75"H
(2) **$275**
Right: **Composition ghoul candy container (opens at bottom)**
Germany
pre-1920s
3"H
(2) **$300**

JOL with stylized hat candy container (hat removes)
Germany
1920s
3"H
(2) **$525**
It has a light compo wash over cardboard.

JOL-headed witch candy container (opens at neck)
Germany
1920s
7.5"H
(3) **$375**
This piece has a composition head and body, crepe hat, corn silk hair, and original twig broom.

Black cat atop JOL candy container (bottom plug)
Germany
1920s
5"H x 3.75"W
(2) **$375**
This figure features a compo cat, wood nose, and a light compo wash over cardboard.

Matched set of composition candy containers (bottom plugs)
Germany
pre-1920s
2"H
(2) **$850 for the set**

▶ **Matched set of composition candy containers (bottom plugs)**
Germany
1920s
3"H
(1) **$1,300 for the set**
The expressions captured on these small items are a hallmark characteristic of the finest in German design.

◀ **JOL mushroom candy container (opens at bottom)**
Germany
1920s
4.25"H
(2) **$575**
It has a light compo wash over cardboard.

◀ **Composition witch head candy container with molded cardboard hat (bottom plug)**
Germany
1920s
5"H
(2) **$525**

◀ **Trio of composition witches**
Germany
1920s
Left: **Figural,** 4.25"H, (3) **$250**
Middle: **Figural,** 5.75"H, (3) **$375**
Right: **Candy Container (opens at bottom),** 3.25"H, (2) **$200**

59

◄ **Two composition devil candy containers**
Germany
1920s
Left: **Opens at bottom**
3.5"H
(3) **$275**
Right: **Bottom plug. Nodder as well**
3.5"H
(2) **$425**

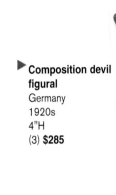

► **Composition devil figural**
Germany
1920s
4"H
(3) **$285**

◄ **Composition devil on a stump candy container (bottom plug)**
Germany
1930s
5"H
(2) **$425**

► **Composition devil head candy container with tongue on a spring (opens at bottom)**
Germany
pre-1920s
3.75"H
(2) **$725**
REPRO ALERT: A large variant of this container (solid mouth, no tongue) is commonly seen, typically without a base. These pieces were among the first wave of German reproductions to hit the United States in the mid 1990s. They have decorative value only.

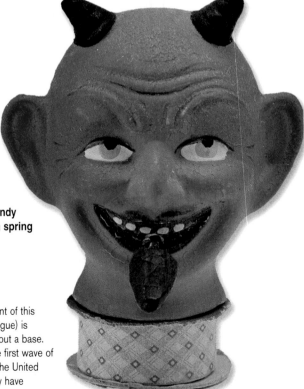

60

◄ **Composition devil head candy container (bottom plug)**
Germany
1920s
3.75"H
(2) **$800**

◄ **Devil candy container (head opens at middle)**
Germany
1920s
12.5"H
(2) **$800**
It features light compo wash over cardboard head, compo shoes, and felt clothing over flexible metal frame. This inspired mixture of differing mediums led to one of the most fanciful of the German creations.

▲ **Devil candy container (opens at bottom)**
Germany
1920s
8.5"H
(2) **$450**
This whimsical container has a light compo wash over cardboard, wood nose, and crepe collar.

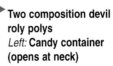

► **Two composition devil roly polys**
Left: **Candy container (opens at neck)**
Germany
pre-1920s
5.5"H x 4"W
(2) **$850**
Right: **Figural with spring horns, weighted by a lead ball**
Germany
early 1930s
(2) **$450**

61

▶ **Composition dancing witch and cat with a spring tail candy container (opens at bottom)**
Germany
1920s
2.75"H
(2) **$475**

▼ **Heavy composition black cat emerging from pumpkin candy container (bottom plug)**
Germany
pre-1920s
2.75"H
(2) **$525**

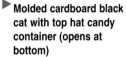

▶ **Molded cardboard black cat with top hat candy container (opens at bottom)**
Germany
1920s
5.5"H
(3) **$250**
REPRO ALERT:
Reproduced versions of this container with varying body and hat colors were made beginning in 2000. The reproductions are more perfectly cylindrical with a much heavier compo wash than vintage items.

◀ **Two composition candy containers**
Germany
1920s
Left: **Opens at bottom**
2.25"H
(3) **$135**
Right: **Bottom plug**
2.5"H
(3) **$165**

◀ **Glazed composition black cat candy container (opens at bottom)**
Germany
1920s
4.5"H
(2) **$375**

▶ **Molded cardboard black cat head candy container (opens at middle)**
Germany, (marked "Container Made in Germany")
1950s
4.5"H x 3"W
(3) **$195**

▲ **Composition black cat pulling pumpkin house candy container (bottom plug)**
Germany
1920s
3.25"H x 3.25"L
(2) **$600**

◀ **Black cat emerging from pumpkin candy container (bottom plug)**
Germany
1920s
6"H x 4"W
(3) **$550**
This container has a light compo wash over molded cardboard pumpkin and a compo cat with a crepe bow tie.
REPRO ALERT: Reproduced versions of this container with a much smaller pumpkin base were made in the mid-1990s. These new versions tend to be heavier and lack the superb detailing of authentic items.

63

◄ **Composition ghost figural "dancer" with spring movement**
Germany
1920s
4.75"H
(2) **$700**
Ghost figural imagery is surprisingly rare. This item typically has a candy box bottom.

▶ **Composition black cat holding pumpkin candy container (bottom plug)**
Germany
1920s
5.5"H
(2) **$525**

▶ **Composition black cat atop a pear candy container (bottom plug)**
Germany
1920s
4.25"H x 3.5"L
(1) **$950**

▲ **Composition witch nodding figural**
Germany
1920s
7"H
(2) **$775**

Molded cardboard black cat nodding candy container with spring tail and spring connector from body to head (bottom plug)
Germany
(marked "Made in US Zone Germany")
1945–1949
5"H x 7"L
(3) **$325**

Composition devil nodder and JOL candy container (bottom plug)
Germany
1920s
5.5"H
(2) **$875**

Composition ghoul nodding figural
Germany
1920s
8.25"H
(2) **$825**

Composition black cat atop a winking harvest moon candy container (bottom plug)
Germany
1920s
5.25"H
(1) **$950**

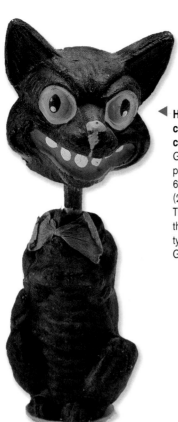

Heavy composition black cat nodding candy container (bottom plug)
Germany
pre-1920s
6.25"H
(2) **$650**
The rich detailing conveying the cat's fur and his ribs are typical of the meticulous German designs.

Composition nodder
Germany
1920s
5"H
(4) **$275**

Composition Veggie creature nodder
Germany
1920s
6"H
(2) **$525**

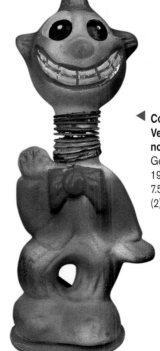

Composition Veggie creature nodder
Germany
1920s
7.5"H
(2) **$675**

◀ **Heavy composition nodder with pipe**
Germany
pre-1920s
5.75"H
(3) **$325**

◀ **Composition English Bobby nodder with big ears**
Germany
1920s
6.25"H
(1) **$800**

◀ **Composition JOL-headed boy nodder**
Germany
1930s
5.25"H
(2) **$475**
This piece has a more sophisticated nodder mechanism than commonly seen.

◀ **Composition JOL-headed woman nodder with pink sunbonnet**
Germany
1920s
7"H
(2) **$650**

67

A NICE VARIETY

The items shown within this section didn't fit easily into other categories, so I thought it would be appropriate to put them together into one chapter. The "Trix or Treats" sucker holder cards are visually interesting and were issued by the prolific E. Rosen Company of Rhode Island, best known for their many hard plastic holiday creations. Most of the decorative candles were manufactured by the seemingly omnipresent Gurley Candle Company of New York. Responsible for many wax designs issued during the 1950s through the 1970s, Gurley candles, as well as those from other makers, are easily found today and comprise an affordable niche for many collectors.

▲ **Trio of Hallowe'en Trix or Treats cardboard sucker holder cards**
USA, E. Rosen Company of Providence, Rhode Island
1948–1950s
4.75"H x 3.75"W
Left: **Scarecrow,** (4) **$35**
Middle: **Owl,** (4) **$35**
Right: **Girl with JOL,** (3) **$40**

▲ **Trio of Hallowe'en Trix or Treats cardboard sucker holder cards**
USA, E. Rosen Company of Providence, Rhode Island
1948–1950s
4.75"H x 3.75"W
Left: **Broomed Witch,** (3) **$40**
Middle: **Pirate Boys,** (4) **$35**
Right: **Cat,** (3) **$45**

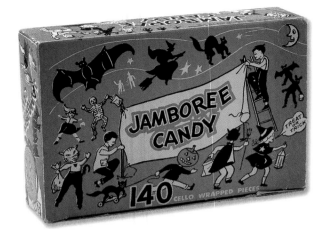

▲ **Jamboree Candy box**
USA, Jamboree Sales Company of Los Angeles, California
1950s
5.75"H x 2"W x 9"L
(3) **$60**

▲ **Hallowe'en Trix or Treats cardboard sucker holder card**
USA, E. Rosen Company of Providence, Rhode Island
late 1950s
3.5"H x 3.25"W
(2) **$50**

▲ **Hallowe'en Witch with Lolly Pops box**
USA, W & F Manufacturing Company of Buffalo, New York
copyrighted 1949
10.5"H x 4"W x 7.25"L
(3) **$65**

▲ **Hallowe'en Decorations box for a set of six German diecuts**
Germany
1920s
15.5"H x 1.5"W x 7.5"L
(2) **$375**
The stock number 2227/234 appears at the lower right.

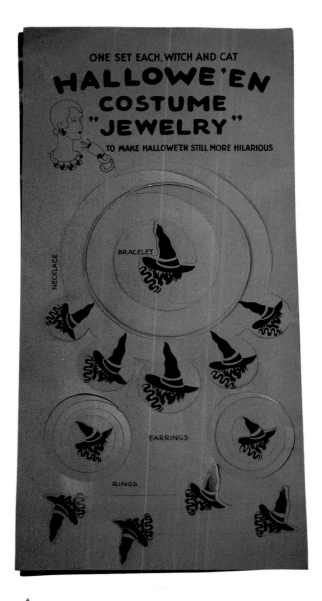

▲ **A Sane Halloween poster**
USA, T.G. Nichols Company of Kansas City, Missouri
copyrighted 1932
16.75"H x 12.5"W
(4) **$70**
It is the eighth in their Character-Culture-Citizenship Guides series of posters.

▲ **Packaged set #529 of 12 small posters to color**
USA, Beckley-Cardy Company of Chicago, Illinois
copyrighted 1950
9"H x 11"W
(3) **$85**

▲ **Hallowe'en Costume "Jewelry" made from thin glossy stock paper**
USA, Dennison, (no mark)
1933
15"H x 7.5"W
(1) **$400 both sets**
Each set (witch faces and cat faces, with only the witches showing here) consists of one necklace, one bracelet, two earrings, and two rings.

Set of three milk glass perfume bottles
Germany
1930s
2"H x 1.75"W
(3) **$225 set**

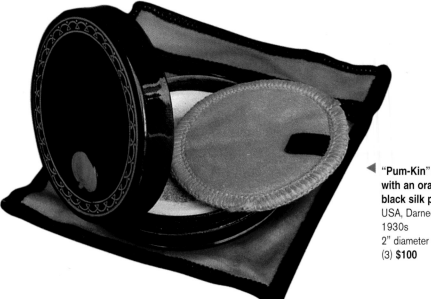

"Pum-Kin" compact with an orange and black silk pouch
USA, Darnee of New York
1930s
2" diameter
(3) **$100**

Pair of plastic cat-faced Fosta Funglasses
USA, Foster Grant Company of Leominster, Massachusetts
1950s
3"H x 6"W
(4) **$35**

Two carded plastic Fosta Funglasses
USA, Foster Grant
Company of Leominster,
Massachusetts
1950s
5.25"H x 6.5"W
(3) **$60 each**

Porcelain skeleton advertising item
Germany
1930s
2.5"H x 4"W
(2) **$175**

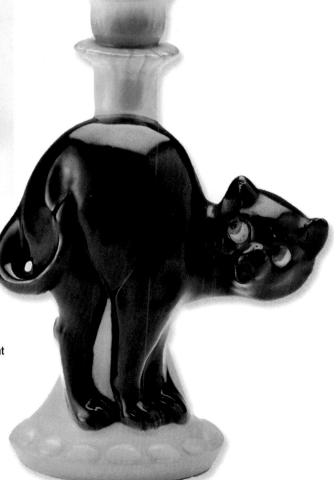

Porcelain black cat candleholder
Germany
pre-1920s
7"H x 5"W
(2) **$325**

◀ **Tin devil face pull toy with movable eyes and tongue**
Germany
pre-1920s
3"H x 2.5"W
(3) **$135**

▼ **Metal red devil face automotive license plate attachment**
USA, National Colortype Company of Bellevue, Kentucky
1920s
5"H x 3.75"W
(2) **$130**

◀ **Porcelain devil creamer**
Germany, Schafer & Vater
1920s
3.25"H x 3.5"W
(3) **$375**

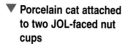 **Porcelain cat attached to two JOL-faced nut cups**
Germany
1920s
3.5"H x 3"W x 4"L
(2) **$325**
This is one piece.

▲ **Porcelain handled tea cup with matching saucer**
Germany
1920s
Cup: 1.25"H x 2"W
(3) **$115**
Saucer: 3.25" diameter
(2) **$165**

▶ **Two metal candleholders**
USA
pre-1920s
7"H x 3.5"W
(2) **$250 each**
These efficiently designed items could be used either for the tabletop or as wall sconces.

A Nice Variety

Porcelain skeleton "Poison" liquor decanter with four skull cups
Japan
1930s
Decanter: 7"H
Cups: 1.75"H
(3) **$225 set**

▲ **JOL-faced matchstick holder made from molded cardboard with a light compo wash**
Germany
1920s
4.5"H x 2"W
(2) **$225**

◀ **Porcelain children's tea set**
Germany
1920s–1935
Lidded teapot: 4"H x 5"W
(2) **$675**
Lidded sugar: 2.5"H x 3.5"W
(3) **$325**
Without lid: **$175**
Creamer: 2.25"H x 2.75"W
(3) **$165**
Waste bowl: 2.25" diameter
(2) **$175**
Cup: 2"H x 2.25"W
(4) **$95 each**
Handled cup: 2"H x 3"W
(2) **$145**

▼ **Fan with differing imagery on each side and an orange honeycomb center**
USA, Beistle, (no mark)
pre-1920s
8.5"H x 2.75"W
(2) **$275**
An arched-back black cat appears on the other side.

▲ **The Beistle Company Fiftieth Anniversary medallion**
USA, Beistle
1950
3" diameter
(3) **$95**

▶ **Metal devil figure with superb detailing**
unknown
pre-1920s
3"H x 6"L
(2) **$280**

◀ **Pair of cardboard stand-up sucker holders**
USA, E. Rosen Company of Providence, Rhode Island
1948
4.5"H x 3.75"W
Left: **Hallowe'en Harry**
(3) **$60**
Right: **Halloween Hattie**
(2) **$90**

▲ **Candles**
USA, Gurley Candle Company of Buffalo, New York
Left: 1950s, 3"H
(5) **$15**
Middle: 1950s, 3"H
(5) **$15**
Right: 1960s, 4"H
(5) **$15**

▼ **Skeleton candle**
USA, Gurley Candle Company of
Buffalo, New York
1960s
8.5"H
(4) **$50**

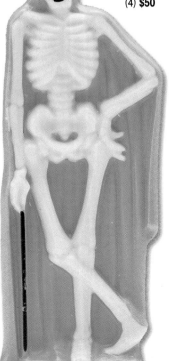

▼ **Matched pair of candleholders with circular cardboard bases, crepe ruffles, and thin paper black cat and JOL diecuts**
USA
early 1950s
3"H x 6"W
(3) **$65 set**

◀ **Candles**
USA, Gurley Candle
Company of Buffalo,
New York
Left: 1950s
3"H
(5) **$15**
Right 1960s
5.5"H
(4) **$30**

Candles
USA, Gurley Candle Company of Buffalo, New York
Left: 1950s, 4"H
(5) **$20**
Middle: 1950s, 2.25"H
(5) **$25**
Right: 1950s, 3.25"H
(5) **$20**

Candles
USA, Gurley Candle Company of Buffalo, New York
Left: 1950s
3.25"H
(5) **$20**
Right: 1950s
3"H
(4) **$25**

Owl candle
USA, Gurley Candle Company of Buffalo, New York
1960s
7.25"H
(4) **$35**

Candles
USA, Gurley Candle Company of Buffalo, New York
Cats: 1950s
3.5"H
(5) **$20 each**
Candlesticks: 1950s
4.5"H
(4) **$20 each**

▲ **JOL candle**
USA, Gurley Candle Company of
Buffalo, New York
1950s
6"H x 5.25"W
(4) **$35**

▲ **Boxed set of three candles**
USA, Gurley Candle Company of Buffalo, New York
1950s
4.25"H x 5"W
(4) **$45**

▶ **JOL candle with box**
USA
late 1940s
Candle:
2.25"H
(4) **$20**
Box:
3" square
(2) **$85**

▼ **Black cat candle**
USA
1940s
7.5"H
(3) **$75**

Four-In-One-Lantern

Although the lantern itself is sometimes seen, the envelope is not. It does shed light on when the lantern was manufactured. Described on the envelope as the "Most Attractive Lantern Made for Decorating Porches, Dining Rooms, and Ball Rooms," it was patented by the Knorpp Candy Company of 56–60 Scholes Street of Brooklyn, New York, on July 11, 1916. The lantern itself only references that a patent has been applied for, so the date on the envelope is significant in expanding our knowledge of this piece, as in *Halloween in America* it had been attributed to around 1940. The envelope measures 7" high by 9.5" wide, with the lantern measuring 6.5" high by 4.75" wide. The four panels of the lantern show a skull, an owl face, a devil face, and a cat face. The two items together are valued at **$375 to $475**.

Mechanical JOL Policeman

Made in Germany in the 1920s, this JOL-faced policeman is termed "mechanical" because when his hat is pushed down, his arms raise up. This is quite an intricate item, standing 8" high. The hat is made from composition, with the head being lithoed paper over cardboard. The hands and feet are wood and the clothing is either felt or wool, with a glossy fabric used for the belt. Great care was taken with the detailing. The stitching of the jacket's cuffs is precise, and small dots of paint were used to simulate jacket buttons! This was an expensive item when it was first manufactured, intended for high-end social gatherings. Consequently, there were few made, and even fewer exist today. This unique item is valued at **$1,600 to $1,800**.

Rookwood Halloween Jardinière

This stunning Rookwood jardinière is the earliest piece in the collection. Made in 1882 near the very beginning of Rookwood's distinguished history, this Limoges style glaze jardinière is decorated with a pair of broomed witches and numerous bats flying by the light of a white moon. If you look closely, you'll see one of the witches has her familiar black cat riding on her broomstick. This jardinière was done by then 18-year-old artist, Albert Humphreys, who worked for Rookwood in Ohio from about 1882 through 1884. Living from 1864 until 1926, Mr. Humphreys had a noted career, with paintings now residing in the Detroit Art Institute, and sculpture in the National Gallery. This jardinière has an elaborate impressed border that encircles the top and bottom and is colored with fired-on gold. Markings on the base include "Rookwood" in block letters, the 1882 date, shape number 95, "Y" denoting yellow clay, an impressed anchor, and the artist's initials. It measures 6.25" high by 9.5" in diameter. This piece was on the market once—in 1882. It was passed down in that same family until early 2002 when it was acquired for this collection. It is valued at **$3,500 to $5,000**.

Diecut Lantern

This rare collapsible eight-panel lantern was made in Germany in the 1920s. It has repeated images of an owl surrounded by bats, as well as a broomed witch, on the four upper panels. The lower panels have repeated images of a JOL with a crow, and an arched-back cat. This is an imposing lantern due its sheer size and detailing. It measures 16" high by 8.25" wide. It is valued at **$800 to $900**.

Mechanicals

These mechanical items were made in Germany before 1920. Both of the items' faces are made from lithoed paper over cardboard. The handles, as well as the arms and legs, are wood. The multi-colored outfits are made from thin cloth. The JOL-creature on the left holds a spun cotton carrot in one hand. Its arms and legs move whenever the ring attached to the bottom of the handle is pulled down. This item measures 10.5" high. The mechanical on the right is more intricate. Whenever the crank at the end of the handle is turned, the figure spins while a tune is played from the central ball. This item measures 13" high. These rare mechanicals are valued at **$1,300 to $1,500 each**.

Pear-Faced Mandolin

This superb pear-faced mandolin came from Germany in the later 1920s. Made with lithoed paper over wood and heavy cardboard with metal strings, it measures 16.25" high by 5.25" at its widest point. Although wholesaler's catalogs make occasional reference to German Halloween mandolins, the dimensions given are far smaller than this piece, so I have long wondered if it was a store display item. It is quite a visually strong piece and stands out wherever it is placed. It is valued at **$4,500 to $6,500**.

Parade Lantern

This is the single best piece in the entire collection. Made in Germany circa, 1908–1912, this layered papier-mâché with compo wash lantern and its original inserts served as the centerpiece of a small town Halloween parade, probably in New Jersey. A stick would be placed in the wooden yoke surrounding the lantern before it was hoisted high to lead the festivities. This item transcends the singular Halloween genre, easily crossing into the wider world of folk art. The design was done by a gifted artist, with the great care taken in its creation, obvious in how dramatic this item truly is to look upon. The Parade Lantern measures 7.25" high by 7.75" diameter and has a removable bottom plug candleholder. This is a one-of-a-kind item as to its size and intended purpose. There are three others known, but they are far smaller, and all were meant for use as tabletop lanterns, as none have yokes. This unique Parade Lantern is valued at **$10,000 to $15,000**.

King Bourbon & Setter Rye Smoke Set

There were 10 of these complete smoke sets made for King Bourbon and Setter Rye as give-aways to their best distributors, sometime from 1891 to 1918. (I tend to think these were made in the earlier half of this range, due to the style of the lettering and glaze.) The sets were made by Schmidt and Company's Victoria Porcelain Factory in Altrohlau, Bohemia. Each piece bears the company's mark in blue, a mark used only during this specific time period. Although many humidors and match holders were made, only 10 plates and 10 ashtrays were produced. The plate reads, "King Bourbon and Setter Rye are Devilish good Whiskies." It measures 9.75" high by 10.25" wide. The match holder (2.25"H x 2.5"W x 3.25"L), ashtray (3"H x 3.75"W x 6.25"L), and lidded humidor (4.75"H x 4.75"W x 5.75"L) all have their original glass eyes. This stunning set has definite crossover appeal to collectors of tobacco and liquor accessories. The set is valued at **$3,000 to $4,000**.

Spook Lamp

This rather primitive item was made in the United States and has a patent date of February 14, 1911. It is made from lithoed paper and medium stock cardboard. The four images on the shade are a JOL, a broomed witch, a bat, and an arched-back black cat. The four images on the base are a witch's hat, a skull and crossbones, a hanging cauldron, and a draped ghoul. The Spook Lamp measures 12" high with a 6" wide shade and a 4.5" wide base. It is valued at **$350 to $450**.

Gibson Party Goods Display Sign

This incredible early 1920s item was a stationery store's display sign for the "Gibson Party Goods for the Hallowe'en Party" line of products. It is large, measuring 28.75" high by 22.75" wide, and made from very heavy cardboard, including its easel. The artwork is stunning, highly stylized, and almost Deco in its execution. The colors are unusual and intense—the background purple contrasting nicely with the gold glow coming from the witch's boiling cauldron. Purple hues don't normally withstand the passage of time well, so this has been a well-cared-for artifact since its creation. The witch has a threatening aura and a face only a warlock could love. This is a highly desirable item, valued at **$1,200 to $1,400**.

Knorpp Candy Company Tiara

This fantastic heavy paper tiara was issued by the Knorpp Candy Company of Brooklyn, New York, and it has a copyright date of 1916. The central devil face is flanked by eight grinning JOLs, which are identical on each side. "Oh You Devil" is printed underneath the central image. This ornately designed tiara measures 5.75" high by 19.75" wide. It is valued at **$350 to $400**.

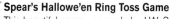

Flaming Hallowe'en Fortune Game

This Flaming Hallowe'en Table Centerpiece and Game with its original glassine envelope and all 12 flaming fortunes was made by Beistle in the early 1930s. It is made from lithoed cardboard with an orange honeycomb base. A typical fortune reads: "Do not worry And do not marry in a hurry." The item measures 6.25" high, without the fortunes, by 7" wide. The envelope measures 9.25" high by 9" wide. It is valued at **$700 to $900**.

Halloween Doll House Lamp

Made in Germany in the early 1920s, this was meant as a seasonal accent piece for a child's dollhouse. It stands 5.5" high with a wood base and central column, an orange silk shade with black piping, and a fringe of numerous glass beads of varying lengths. A composition JOL face is affixed to the shade. It also has its original cord and plug. It is valued at **$600 to $700**.

Spear's Hallowe'en Ring Toss Game

This beautiful game was made by J.W. Spear and Sons of Bavaria sometime around 1910. This is a simple ring toss game, but with exquisite art and presentation. A decorative white clay pipe would be placed in a hole in the JOL's mouth. (There are two pipes with the game.) According to the instructions tipped in inside the box lid, players would stand a fair distance away and attempt to toss the cardboard rings onto the clay pipe. There are 15 rings in a variety of pastel colors. The heavy cardboard JOL face has an easel, as well as a hanging hole, and measures 10" high by 8" wide. The well-constructed and heavy box measures 14.25" high by 1.5" wide by 9.25" long. This is the only such game known to exist. Interestingly, it is stated on the instructions that this is the "Large Edition," naturally begging the question as to whether a "Small Edition" exists. The game is valued at **$2,500 to $3,000**.

▲ German Hallowe'en Fortune Wheel w/Envelope

Because of how this game was meant to be used, only a very few complete examples are known. There is a central disk from which 12 JOLs with differing expressions protrude. The game would be placed on a wall, spun, and players would actually pluck a JOL off to read the fortune printed on the back, according to these instructions: "Pick A Pumpkin and on its back You'll find your future bright or black." Each JOL was numbered and possessed a completely different fortune, all of which were pleasant. A sample fortune reads: "A golden ring, a wedding trip, A mate with love sincere; These three will come, without a slip, And all within a year." The imagery is quite compelling. A very serious looking witch stares out at you while pointing into a book held by a Pixie. This Pixie stares off to one side as if something unseen is approaching. Rounding out the scene is a nervous black cat, bats flying by a barren tree, an owl perching on a branch against a yellow moon, and a smoking cauldron casting a spooky glow. Every other example of this game I have seen was made in the United States. The example in this collection states that it was "Printed in Germany" right above the owl. Additionally, the envelope states that it was "Made in Germany."

Schneider's *Halloween in America* dates this piece to 1916, but I believe it actually is dated from the early 1920s. Here is what I believe is an accurate history of this game: Like several other items marked "Printed in Germany," I believe this was originally commissioned by the Beistle Company during this time frame using German artisans under contract to it for the overall design. (This may be the earliest example of this association, which was definitely over by 1930.) After a single season, Beistle began printing them in the United States, which accounts for the extreme rarity of the German version. (Aside from the German mark, the only difference I have noted between this German example and the American examples I have personally seen is that the former's colors are much deeper and more lush.) This game appears on page 10 of the 1925–1926 Shackman's catalog. It also appears on page 16 of an undated Shackman's catalog alongside a Beistle item that was only made from 1928–1931. This evidence causes me to think that the German item was made in 1923, with Beistle printing them in the United States starting in 1924. Wholesalers like Shackman began selling them in 1925 and continued to do this for perhaps three to four more years. This complete German game with the original paper envelope is valued at **$1,900 to $2,200**.

▶ The Rustic Fireplace

One of the most interesting of Beistle's many tabletop decorations is its Rustic Fireplace. It is billed on the envelope as including an "Old Witches' Beauty Caldron." It consists of a lithoed paper and honeycomb cauldron with orange streamers attached to the bottom to simulate flames. (This was an ingenious way to boost sales of an already popular item.) Since these cauldrons were only made from 1926 through 1931, it stands to reason the Rustic Fireplace dates to this time. This is further buttressed by the use of Beistle's diamond mark on the packaging. The detailed lithoed cardboard props and crossbar containing a hook for the cauldron are all representative of Beistle's high quality. These measure 10.5" high by 15" wide. The cauldron measures 8" high by 8.5" wide. This complete set is valued at **$1,000 to $1,200**.

▲ **Candy Boxes**

This very rare assortment of boxes was made by the E. Rosen Company of Providence, Rhode Island. In the center is a box from the 1950s that once contained 45 Trix or Treats cards, 45 Pops, and nine Moon Pop packages. It measures 5.25"H x 3.25"W x 9"L.

On top of it is a mechanical Moon Pop sucker holder. Part of the witch's cape is a flap that can move up or down. This holder measures 4.75" high by 5" wide. This set is valued at **$225 to $325.**

On the left is a Pumpkin Pops mechanical store display from the 1940s. When the cat is moved back and forth, the eyes roll and the tongue wags. It measures 9"H x 1.5"W x 7.25"L and is valued at **$400 to $500**.

Next is a Spook Pops mechanical store display from the 1940s. When the house is moved back and forth, ghosts along the path to the haunted house pop up. It measures 8.5"H x 1.5"W x 7.25"L and is valued at **$450 to $550**.

On the right is an Owl Pops mechanical store display from the 1940s. When the owl's hat is pushed down, the wings flap and the tail feathers move. It measures 8.75"H x 1.5"W x 7.25"L and is valued at **$400 to $500**.

▶ **1909 Dennison Bogie Book**

Among all of the nearly annual Dennison Bogie Books, this is THE Holy Grail. The first ever, this 1909 edition is never seen. Measuring 8" high by nearly 6.25" wide, it has 16 numbered pages. Very nicely illustrated and profuse with ideas for the proper Halloween party, this Bogie Book was the first step on the road in Dennison's quest to dominate the holiday party niche. Interestingly, Dennison didn't follow up with the next Bogie Book until 1912. Along with the Bogie Book itself is the original mailing envelope and an order form listing the five Dennison stores open at that time: Boston, New York, Philadelphia, Chicago, and St. Louis. The three items together are valued at **$1,400 to $1,600.**

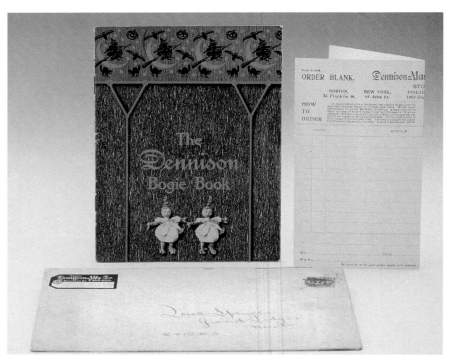

Carnival Chalkware "Holloween" Boy

Chalkware prizes were very popular on the nation's carnival midways primarily from the 1920s through the 1940s. They were all cheaply made and quickly painted. Because of their inherent fragility, it's surprising that any exist today. Few are as sought after as this very compelling figure of a boy wearing a dunce-like hat (perhaps for misspelling Halloween as Holloween on his hat), a mask, and holding a JOL. Although there were numerous color variations made, all are equally rare and desirable. He stands 15.75" high and is 7.75" wide. This item is valued at **$1,700 to $1,900**.

Pulp Witches

Both of these pulp witches were made in the US in the 1930s. The taller witch measures 9" high and is valued at **$400 to $500**. The witch sitting by her cauldron was probably made by the F.N. Burt Company of Buffalo, New York. It measures 4.75" high by 3" wide and is valued at **$350 to $450**.

Devil Face Tambourine

This tambourine was made in Japan in the 1930s. It measures 6.5" in diameter and is made from banded wood with a taut glazed paper face. It originally had three tin bells, of which two survive. It is valued at **$575 to $675**.

Pumpkin Garland Envelope

This cardboard envelope for a Pumpkin Garland Decoration was made by Beistle in the 1920s. The envelope measures 6.5" high by 11.5" wide and is valued at **$250 to $350**. Early Beistle packaging is extremely desirable as the company expended effort to make the packaging quite compelling and attractive.

Tin Banjo

Although sparsely decorated, this banjo is quite well-made from a combination of tin, wood, and wire. It measures 9.75" high by 3" wide. Not marked, the banjo was almost certainly made in the United States in the 1930s and is valued at **$650 to $750**.

▼ Champagne Bucket Candy Container

An appealingly designed candy container, this was made in Germany in the 1920s. It measures 3.25" high. The bottom slides out in order to place the candy inside the bucket. Interestingly, inside the bucket rests a bottle of French champagne, La Veuve Clicquot. This novelty candy container is valued at **$1,300 to $1,500**.

▶ Winking JOL Candy Container

This candy container, bursting with personality, was made in Germany in the late teens. It is made from composition and opens from the bottom with a light cardboard plug. It measures 4.5" high by 3" wide. This is one of my favorite candy containers, primarily because of the superb expression. The bit of felt on the nose is not original, but was placed there by a prior owner to hide a surface chip. The open eye has also been lightly repainted, again by that same owner. This container, with its superb design, exemplifies why German items are so highly sought after. This is quite a desirable container, with few, if any, other examples known. It is valued at **$1,900 to $2,100**.

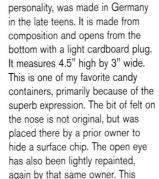

▶ German Cat-in-the-Box

This primitive toy was made in Germany before 1920. It consists of lithoed paper over wood and a crepe-ruffled composition cat's head on a spring. Because these were not particularly sturdy, few have survived. With the lid closed, it measures 3.25" high by 3.5" wide. It is valued at **$600 to $800**.

▲ Candlestick Candy Container

This candy container was made in Germany in the 1920s. It is made from lithoed paper over cardboard, as were all other pieces from this set. (See the Candy Containers, Nodders, and Figurals section.) The candle cover lifts off so that the candy can be placed inside. This item measures 5" high with the base measuring 4.25" in diameter. This container is valued at **$1,200 to $1,300**.

Candy Container Trio

This complete set was made in Germany in the early 1920s with molded cardboard bottoms and composition heads. The heads are removable so that candies can be placed inside. Each measures 8" high. Interestingly, all of the bottoms are the same, merely painted differently, an early example of extracting manufacturing efficiencies from even the simplest of operations. This set, which has been together since manufacture, is exceedingly rare, especially in this condition. This set is valued at **$5,000 to $7,500**.

Devil Nodder

Most nodders, because of their inherent fragility, haven't withstood the passage of time well. This is even truer for the larger, more ornate nodders. This item is an exception to that general truth. It is composition with a painted wood base and stands 8.25" high. The expression on its face is one of supreme contentment. It is valued at **$1,700 to $1,900**.

JOL Admiral Candy Container

Made in Germany in the very early 1920s, this imposing candy container, opening at the neck, measures 9.25" high. It is composition and sits on a painted wood base. This container is a superbly detailed piece, with the admiral even carrying a small telescope. It is valued at **$1,700 to $1,900**.

Set of Faux Stained Glass Diecuts

This complete set of faux stained glass diecuts was manufactured in the early 1920s, probably by Dennison. Made with multi-colored paper surrounded by heavy black cardboard rims, few of these have weathered time well. The colors used: green, purple, and orange are prone to fading. Since they were designed to have a light shine from behind them, it is astonishing that this set has survived with its robust colors intact. They were time-consuming and therefore expensive to manufacture. I also believe they were market flops, due primarily to the coloring and shape of each diecut, which conjures thoughts of a Gothic cathedral. These factors almost certainly caused this experimental set to be made for merely a single season. Each measures 11.5" high by 8.5" wide. The cat and witch are valued at **$900 to $1,000 each**, whereas the boy and the house are valued at **$700 to $800 each**.

Jointed Pumpkin Man Diecut– Early Iteration

This richly detailed and jointed Pumpkin Man was made in the early 1920s. Although it is not marked except for a "Made in U.S.A." printed notation, the piece was made by Beistle, as it has all of the characteristics of its artwork. It is a non-embossed diecut, measuring 19.5" high by 17.25" wide when the arms are fully extended. The abdomen measures 6.25" wide. This is a definite precursor to the more fully rendered and lushly colored item shown below, and as such, constitutes a previously unknown iteration of an already highly sought-after and early Beistle item. It is valued at **$700 to $800.**

Jointed Pumpkin Man Diecut– Later Iteration

This jointed Pumpkin Man was made perhaps a season or two after the earlier iteration (shown above) and shows a definite growth in the artistic capabilities of Beistle's design department. Although the basic features have remained unchanged, this later version is more robustly rendered, as evidenced by the richer coloration, the width of the abdomen, and the additional foliage directly underneath the abdomen. This iteration also has only a "Made in U.S.A." printed notation with no Beistle mark, which is puzzling, as it is clearly one of their earlier masterworks. This non-embossed item measures 21" high by 18.25" wide when the arms are fully extended. The abdomen measures 7.25" wide. It is valued at **$700 to $800.**

Jointed Devil Diecut

This rather grim-looking jointed devil was made in the very early 1920s. Although it is not marked, it was made by Beistle, as a very similar, but later "dancer" is pictured in a 1930 catalog. It is a non-embossed diecut that measures 17.5" high by 17.5" wide when the legs are fully extended. It is valued at **$400 to $500.**

Hobo Cat Diecut

This diecut was made in Germany in the early 1930s. It has unusual flaps that fold out to form a base. Heavily embossed, it measures 9" high by 8" wide and is valued at **$1,000 to $1,200.**

Honeycomb cat face continental hat with plume
USA, Beistle, (printed name)
1925–1931
8.25"H x 14.75"W
(2) **$175**

Broomed witch honeycomb band hat
USA, Beistle, (no mark)
1921
8.5"H x 11.5"W
(2) **$65**

Owl in cauldron honeycomb band hat
USA, Beistle, (no mark)
1921
8.5"H x 11.5"W
(2) **$65**

Honeycomb JOL continental hat with plume
USA, Beistle, (printed name)
1925–1931
6.75"H x 14"W
(2) **$165**

Frightened cat honeycomb band hat with plumes
USA, Beistle, (no mark)
1930s
6.5"H x 11.5"W
(2) **$80**

Electrified cat honeycomb band hat
USA, Beistle, (no mark)
1930s
6"H x 11.5"W
(2) **$100**

DECORATIONS

Packages of 18 matboard imps and witches
USA, Dennison
1912–1915
2.5" square
(2) **$50 each**

Packages of Halloween seals in glassine envelopes
USA, Dennison
1930s
3"H x 3.75"W
(3) **$35 each**

Left: **Box of 20 JOL policeman seals**
USA, Dennison, 1930s, 3"H x 1.75"W, (2) **$65**
Middle: **Envelope of 12 black cat cut-outs #H32**
USA, Dennison, pre-1920s, 3"H x 3.5"W, (3) **$45**
Right: **Box of 6 face-on-leaf gummed seals**
USA, Dennison, first appeared in the 1924 Bogie Book,
3.75"H x 2.25"W, (3) **$65**

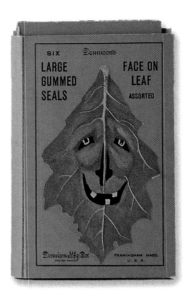

Left: **Box of 12 gummed witch silhouettes**
USA, Dennison, first appeared in the 1929 Parties magazine
2.5"H x 3.5"W, (3) **$65**

Middle: **Box of 6 owl silhouettes**
USA, Dennison, first appeared in the 1926 Bogie Book
5"H x 3.25"W, (3) **$70**

Right: **Box of 6 JOL cut-outs #H-96**
USA, Dennison, first appeared in the 1923 Bogie Book, 4" square, (4) **$60**

Left: **Box of 15 cat head seals**
USA, Dennison, 1930s, 2"H x 3"W, (4) **$40**

Middle: **Box of 20 cat head seals (#H-654)**
USA, Dennison, 1923–1924, 2"H x 3.25"W, (3) **$55**

Right: **Box of 25 cat head seals**
USA, Dennison, 1920s, 1.5"H x 2.5"W, (3) **$50**

Left: **Box of 25 girl and spook seals (#H-637)**
USA, Dennison, 1922–1924, 1.5"H x 2.5"W, (2) **$65**

Middle: **Box of 25 crescent moon gummed decorations (#13)**
USA, Dennison, first appeared in the 1921 Bogie Book, 2" square
(4) **$10**

Right: **Box of 25 owl and elf seals (#H-635)**
USA, Dennison, 1922–1923, 1.5"H x 2.5"W, (2) **$65**

▶ *Left:* **Box of 6 witch place cards (#H-1)**
USA, Dennison
1912–1915
2.25"H x 4.5"W
(2) **$125**

Middle: **Box of 6 owl cut-outs (#H-99)**
USA, Dennison
1920s
4"H x 3.25"W
(3) **$55**

Right: **Box of 12 JOL cut-outs for ices (#H-20)**
USA, Dennison
1915–1917
4"H x 2"W
(2) **$125**

▼ *Ends:* **Boxes of 20 leaf monster seals**
USA, Dennison, 1930s, 1.5"H x 2.5"W, (3) **$45 each**
Middle Left: **Box of 20 JOL/owl seals**
USA, Dennison, first appeared in the 1929 Parties magazine
2.5"H x 2"W, (3) **$60**
Middle Right: **Box of 25 bandit JOL seals**
USA, Dennison, 1920s, 1.25"H x 2"W, (2) **$65**

▼ *Left:* **Box of 25 wizard at cauldron seals**
USA, Dennison, 1920s, 1.5"H x 2"W, (2) **$65**
Middle: **Box of 10 black cat cut-outs**
USA, Dennison, 1930s, 3"H x 2.25"W, (3) **$40**
Right: **Box of 20 witch in cauldron seals**
USA, Dennison, 1920s, 1.5"H x 2.5"W, (2) **$70**

Left: **Box of 20 witch at cauldron seals**
USA, Dennison, 1930s, 2"H x 2.5"W, (2) **$75**
Middle: **Box of 20 cat in moon seals**
USA, Dennison, 1931, 2.75"H x 2"W, (2) **$55**
Right: **Box of 25 haunted house seals**
USA, Dennison, 1930s, 1.5"H x 2.5"W, (3) **$60**

Left: **Box of 18 broomed witch illuminated silhouettes (#458)**
USA, Dennison, 1912–1915, 2.25"H x 3"W, (2) **$120**
Middle: **Box of 6 broomed witch gummed silhouettes**
USA, Dennison, 1927–1928, 4"H x 5"W, (3) **$75**
Right: **Box of 50 broomed witch illuminated silhouettes (#440)**
USA, Dennison, 1912–1915, 2"H x 2.25"W, (2) **$80**

Grouping of "Party Helps"
USA, Beistle, (stated on envelopes)
1920s, 5"H x 4"W, (3) **$85 each**
Left: **Envelope with 10 cat head cut-outs**
Middle: **Envelope with 13 silhouette seals**
Right: **Envelope with 6 tally cards (#513)**

DECORATIONS

▲ **An assortment of seals**
USA, Gibson Art Company of Cincinnati, Ohio, 1930s
From Left: **Box of 20 owl seals,** 1.75"H x 1.25"W, (3) **$35**
    Box of 12 owl and moon seals, 2"H x 1.5"W, (3) **$35**
    Box of 20 broomed witch seals, 1.25"H x 1.75"W, (3) **$40**
    Box of 20 JOL with knife seals, 2" square, (3) **$30**

▲ *Left:* **Box of 20 owl seals**
USA, Gibson Art Company of Cincinnati, Ohio,
1930s, 1.75"H x 1.5"W, (3) **$25**
Middle: **Box of 12 cat head seals**
USA, Gibson Art Company of Cincinnati, Ohio,
1930s, 1.75" square, (3) **$25**
Right: **Box of 20 cat seals**
USA, Gibson Art Company of Cincinnati, Ohio,
1920s, 2"H x 1.5"W, (2) **$45**

▶ **Box of 48 witch seals**
USA, Whitney Company of
Worcester, Massachusetts
1920s
1.75"H x 1.25"W
(2) **$45**

▶ **Envelope with 9 assorted cat head seals and decorating tips sheet (#760-C)**
USA, Beistle, (diamond mark)
1925–1930
5.25"H x 4.25"W
(2) **$115**

▲ **Envelope with 5 fortune place cards**
USA, Beistle, (no mark)
1920s
5"H x 4"W
(3) **$75**

▲ *Left:* **Box of 14 silhouette cut-out decorations**
USA, Beistle, (no mark), 1920s, 5.25"H x 4.5"W, (3) **$85**
Right: **Box of 25 assorted silhouettes**
USA, Beistle, (diamond mark), 1925–1930, 7.25"H x 5.75"W, (3) **$110**

▶ **Envelope with 6 cut-out silhouette decorations (#747)**
USA, Beistle, (no mark)
1920s
5.25"H x 4.5"W
(3) **$60**

▲ **Envelope with 24 fortune verses**
USA, Whitney Company of Worcester, Massachusetts
1920s
3.5"H x 6.5"W
(3) **$35**
The contents are simply 4 sheets with 6 fortunes each.

▲ **Box of 12 spinning place cards with fortunes**
USA, Whitney Company of Worcester, Massachusetts
1920s
4"H x 6"W
(2) **$65**
The contents are 12 place cards and wooden spindles, plus 2 sheets with 6 fortunes each.

DECORATIONS

▲ **Envelope with 10 assorted silhouettes**
USA, Beistle, (no mark)
1920s
11.25"H x 6.75"W
(4) **$75**

▲ **Envelope with 5 "mechanical" invitations (#597)**
USA, Beistle, (very early "B Co" mark)
1921
7.25"H x 5"W
(2) **$125 set**
The movable part on each card is primitively attached
with a simple metal rivet.

► **A pair of stand-up place cards
with running mice along the
bottom borders**
USA, Whitney Company of
Worcester, Massachusetts
1920s
4.25"H x 3"W
(3) **$45 each**

▼ **A pair of pop-up party invitations**
USA, Beistle, (no mark)
1920s
6.25"H x 6"W
(3) **$40 each**

▲ **Bridge tally and score card set
with honeycomb tutus**
USA, Beistle, (diamond mark)
1930–1931
5.5"H x 2.75"W
(2) **$130 for the set**

▲ **Bridge tally card**
USA, Beistle, (diamond mark)
1925–1930
5"H x 3.5"W
(2) **$60**
The apron flips up to reveal the scoring area. There is
a penciled notation on the reverse indicating this was
used at a party on October 22, 1929.

Complete set of 6 place cards
USA, (probably Whitney)
1930s
3.75"H x 4.25"W
(2) $95 for the set
Each cat's and moon's expression is different. The sides bend inward to make each card stand.

Place card
USA, Dennison
1926–1928
2.75"H x 3.5"W
(2) $25

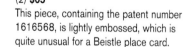

Place card with flip-out base
USA, Beistle, (diamond mark)
1925–1930
3"H x 4"W x 4"L
(2) $65
This piece, containing the patent number 1616568, is lightly embossed, which is quite unusual for a Beistle place card.

Placecard and table decoration
USA, Dennison
late 1920s
Left: **Place card**
3"H x 3.25"W
(3) $35
Right: **Table decoration**
6.25"H x 5.75"W
(3) $60
The artwork on this matched set is compelling. Notice the cat face in the flames, the candles' expressions, and how the cats along the base of the larger item skew to give the effect of a rounded base.

DECORATIONS

115

▶ **Pair of nut cups**
USA, Merri-Lei Company of Brooklyn, New York
1948–1955
3.75"H x 1"W x 3"L
(4) **$20 each**
One characteristic of most of this company's products was the glossy heavy paper stock used, as demonstrated by these items.

▲ **Set of 10 paper doilies with original glassine envelope**
USA
1920s
6"H x 6.5"W
(2) **$20 per doily**

▲ **Set of 10 paper doilies with original glassine envelope**
USA
1920s
6"H x 6.5"W
(2) **$20 per doily**

▶ *Left:* **Package of 24 Linen paper doilies**
USA, Dennison
1920s
6.25" square
(2) **$15 per doily**
Right: **Package of 24 linen paper doilies**
USA, Dennison
1920s
8.25" square
(2) **$20 per doily**

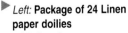

▲ **Trio of nut cups**
USA, Dolly Toy Company of
Tipp City, Ohio
1950s
2.5"H x 1.5"W x 2"L
(3) **$25 each**

▲ **Complete set of 4 nut cups**
USA, Dennison
late 1920s
1.5"H x 1.5" to 2"W x 2.5" to 3.25"L
(2) **$40 each**
The liberal use of gold coloring is
unusual.

▲ **Set of 4 witch nut cups/place cards**
USA, (probably Whitney)
1930s
3"H x 1.75"W x 2"L
(3) **$25 each**
Although these are printed on both sides,
they can be correctly assembled only one
way.

The evolution in the design of the dancers from 1928–1964 illustrates the point that as artwork is done closer to our modern day, the imagery is generally less threatening, therefore becoming more salable to greater numbers of consumers.

Witch dancer
USA, Beistle, (no mark)
1948–1964
7"W with varying lengths
(5) **$25**

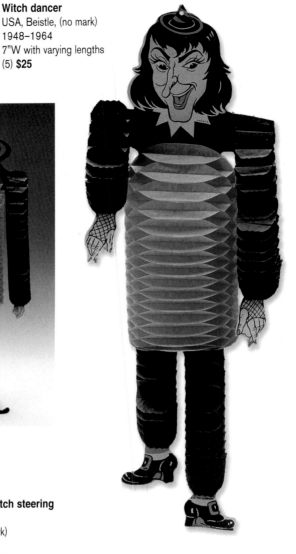

Witch dancer
USA, Beistle, (no mark)
1938–1946
7.5"W with varying lengths
(4) **$40**

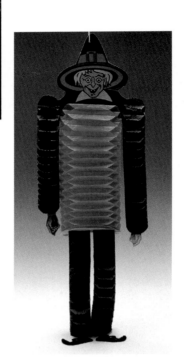

◄ **Identically-sided witch steering a flying saucer**
USA, Beistle, (no mark)
1956–1961
11.25"H x 15"W x 16"L
(4) **$45**

▶ **Identically-sided witch steering a flying sauce**
USA
1960s
11.25"H x 14.5"W x 15"L
(5) **$25**

Cat dancer
USA, Beistle, (no mark)
1938–1946
7"W with varying lengths
(4) **$40**
Originally made on a lark from scrap materials in the late 1920s, dancers of all varieties became long-time big sellers for Beistle.

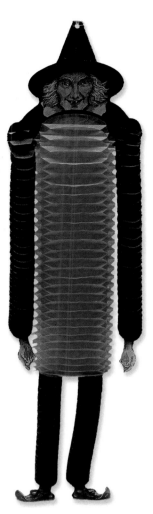

Witch dancer
USA, Beistle, (diamond mark)
1928–1937
7"W with varying lengths
(3) **$80**
Only items from the first years of production have the diamond mark. Later iterations will have no mark. This difference alone should have no bearing on value.

Cat dancer
USA, Beistle, (no mark)
1948–1964
7"W with varying lengths
(5) **$25**

Cat dancer
USA, Beistle, (no mark)
1928–1937
6.25"W with varying lengths
(3) **$95**
Even without the help of catalogs, it is apparent this is an older dancer design due to the fine detailing. The "Made in USA" mark also supports this conclusion. Only items from the first years of production have the diamond mark. Later iterations will have no mark, as in this case. This difference alone should have no bearing on value.

119

▲ **Five nut cups**
USA, Dennison, 1920s
From Left: 2"H x 1.75"W x 2.25"L, (4) **$20**
1.5"H x 2.25"W x 2.25"L, (3) **$30**
1.5"H x 2.25"W x 2.25"L, (3) **$30**
1.25"H x 2.25"W x 1.5"L, (3) **$25**
1.5"H x 2.25"W x 2.25"L, (3) **$30**

▲ **Pumpkin, owl, and cat**
Left: **Pulp JOL nut cup**
USA, 1950s, 2.5"H, (5) **$40**
Middle: **Pulp owl decoration**
USA, 1950s, 3.5"H, (4) **$40**
Right: **Pulp cat**
USA, late 1940s, 3.5"H x 3.75"W, (4) **$50**

▲ **Witch silhouette against honeycomb moon**
USA, Beistle, (no mark)
1960–1962
17.5" in diameter
(2) **$35**

▲ **Pair of reversible nut cups/place cards**
USA, Beistle, (no mark)
appears in their 1948 catalog
3.5"H x 1.75"W x 3.5"L
(3) **$30 each**
Each side has the differing imagery shown, with the
containers fitted together by interlocking ends.

DECORATIONS

Identically-sided 3-D flying owl
USA, The Gibson Art Company of
Cincinnati, Ohio
1930s
7"H x 6.75"W x 11.5"L
(3) **$65**
A smaller version otherwise identical
was made and is much more rare. It
measures 7"L.

**Package of 6 identically-sided, light
cardboard "wriggling snakes"**
USA, Beistle, (no mark)
1920s
Package: 11.5"H x 6.5"W
Snake: 6" in diameter x 3' long
(2) **$150 set**

JOL "hot foot dancer"
USA, Beistle, (HE Luhrs mark)
1939–1947
40"H x 12"W
(2) **$80**

DECORATIONS

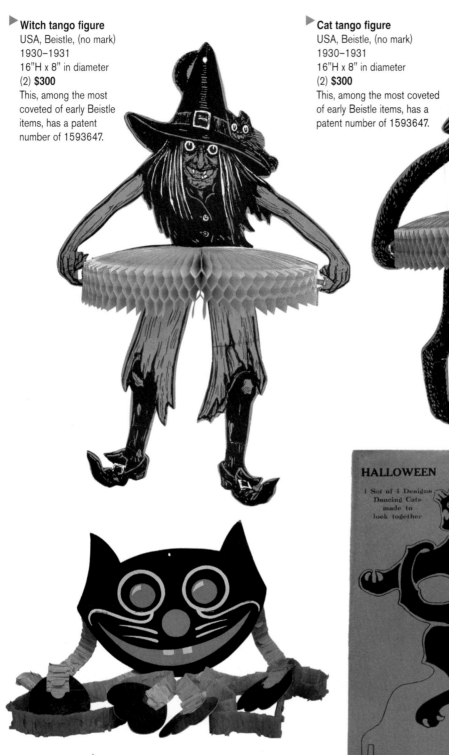

▶ **Witch tango figure**
USA, Beistle, (no mark)
1930–1931
16"H x 8" in diameter
(2) **$300**
This, among the most coveted of early Beistle items, has a patent number of 1593647.

▶ **Cat tango figure**
USA, Beistle, (no mark)
1930–1931
16"H x 8" in diameter
(2) **$300**
This, among the most coveted of early Beistle items, has a patent number of 1593647.

▲ **Cat face "hot foot dancer"**
USA, Beistle, (HE Luhrs mark)
1939–1947
40"H x 12"W
(2) **$100**

▲ **Envelope containing 4 light cardboard interlocking dancing cats that form a centerpiece**
USA
1930s
7.5"H x 6.25"W
(3) **$130**

DECORATIONS

▼ Set of 4 light cardboard interlocking
identical sides that form a broomed
witch centerpiece
USA, (probably Whitney)
1930s
7.75"H x 9"W
(2) **$115 set**

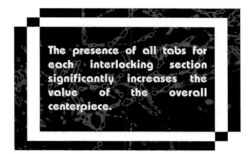

The presence of all tabs for each interlocking section significantly increases the value of the overall centerpiece.

▲ Set of 4 light cardboard interlocking sides
that form a Veggie-people centerpiece
USA
pre-1920s
From Left: 6"H x 5.75"W
6.25"H x 5.25"W
6.25"H x 5.25"W
6"H x 4.75"W

(2) **$145 for the set**

▲ Set of 4 light cardboard
interlocking sides that form a witch
and ghost centerpiece
USA, (probably Whitney)
1930s
8.5" to 9.5"H x 9"W
(2) **$175 set**

DECORATIONS

123

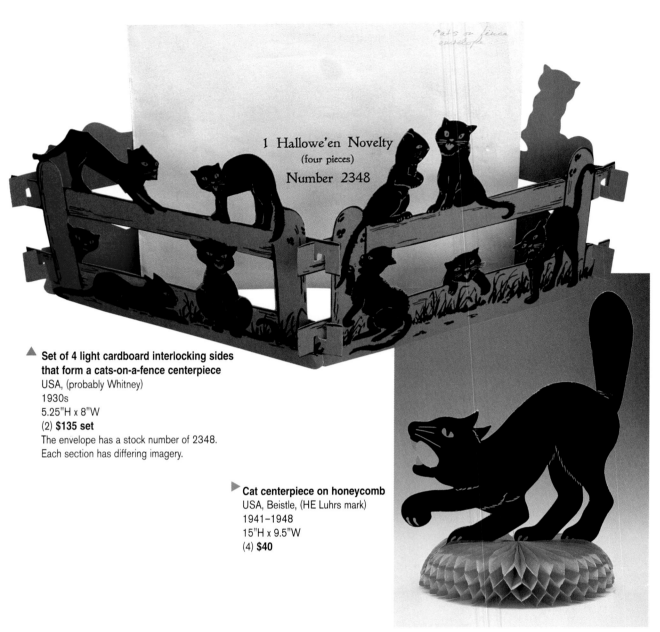

1 Hallowe'en Novelty
(four pieces)
Number 2348

▲ **Set of 4 light cardboard interlocking sides that form a cats-on-a-fence centerpiece**
USA, (probably Whitney)
1930s
5.25"H x 8"W
(2) **$135 set**
The envelope has a stock number of 2348.
Each section has differing imagery.

▶ **Cat centerpiece on honeycomb**
USA, Beistle, (HE Luhrs mark)
1941–1948
15"H x 9.5"W
(4) **$40**

◀ **Set of 4 light cardboard interlocking identical sides that form a singing cats centerpiece**
USA
1940s
5" to 6"H x 9.75"W
(2) **$145 set**

Owl with honeycomb center and back prop
USA, Beistle, (no mark)
1960–1965
14"H x 5"W x 13.25"L
(5) **$35**

▼ Winged ghost table decoration
USA, Beistle, (no mark)
1925–1931
11.5"H x 20"W
(2) **$200**
This item has an easel and would have originally had sheet knots at either side of its head. These knots are invariably missing. The tissue wings are generally orange. This variation possesses a somewhat higher value.

Scarecrow with honeycomb center and back prop
USA, Beistle, (no mark)
1960–1965
14"H x 5"W x 13.25"L
(5) **$35**

▲ 3-D table decoration with honeycomb cauldron
USA, Beistle, (no mark)
1957–1958
9"H x 4"W x 6.5"L
(2) **$100**
The cauldron was also made with orange honeycomb.

129

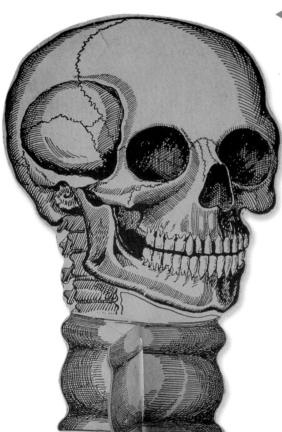

◄ **Skull table decoration with a flip-out base**
USA, Beistle, (diamond mark)
1925–1930
10"H x 4"W x 6"L
(2) **$135**
This was not one of Beistle's best-executed items and it was probably not a best-seller. The art is flat and uninspiring. However, it is this rejection by the marketplace that makes the item rare, and therefore desirable. It has a patent number of 1616568.

► **Pete the Party Puss: The Purrfect Party Promoter**
USA, Beistle, (no mark)
1953–1957
10.5"H x 6.75"W
(3) **$75**
Pete has an easel.

◄ **JOL table decoration with a flip-out base**
USA, Beistle, (no mark)
1925–1930
9.25"H x 3.75"W x 6.75"L
(2) **$155**

DECORATIONS

Pulp owl decoration
USA
1950s
7"H x 4"W x 5"L
(3) **$45**

Jitterbug Jones table decoration
USA
1930s
13.75"H x 7.25"W
(2) **$180**
This item, with an easel, is an early example of glow-in-the-dark party products. The attached placard, generally missing, reads, "I'm Jitterbug Jones, the dancing Bones–Turn off the light, I'll glow all night!" An interesting design element is the cigarette, which lends the overall image an unintended irony.

Heavy pulp owl decoration
USA
1940s
13.25"H x 6"W x 8.25"L
(3) **$80**

Pulp owl decoration
USA, (probably the F. N. Burt Company of Buffalo, New York)
1930s
9.5"H x 4"W x 5.5"L
(3) **$90**

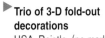

▶ **Trio of 3-D fold-out decorations**
USA, Beistle, (no mark)
late 1940s–1950s
8"H x 2"W x 7.75"L
(4) **$60 each**

▶ **Complete set of 6 table decorations**
USA, Beistle, (no mark)
late 1950s
7" to 10.5"H x 5" to 9.25"W
(4) **$20 each**

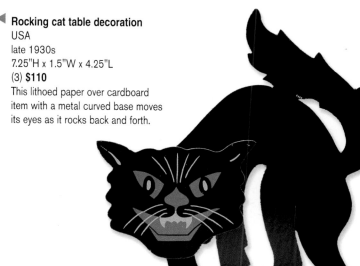

Rocking cat table decoration
USA
late 1930s
7.25"H x 1.5"W x 4.25"L
(3) **$110**
This lithoed paper over cardboard item with a metal curved base moves its eyes as it rocks back and forth.

3-D black cat table decoration
USA, Beistle, (HE Luhrs mark)
1940s
15"H x 3.25"W x 12"L
(2) **$135**
The front legs fit into two slots in the base, and the head is on a flap that can move away from the body, giving this item a simple 3-D effect.

3-D black cat stand-up
USA, Beistle, (HE Luhrs mark)
1940s
20"H x 3.5"W x 8.5"L
(3) **$100**
The head is on a flap that can move away from the body, and the front legs pull away from the back legs, allowing the item to stand and providing a simple 3-D effect.

3-D black cat stand-up
USA, Beistle, (HE Luhrs mark)
1940s
16.5"H x 3.5"W x 8.75"L
(2) **$135**
The front legs pull away from the back legs, allowing the item to stand and providing a simple 3-D effect.

3-D black cat with bow tie corner decoration
USA, Beistle, (HE Luhrs mark)
1940s
18.5"H x 3"W x 13.25"L
(2) **$170**
The front legs pull away from the back legs, allowing the item to stand and providing a simple 3-D effect.

▶ **String-Em-Outs**
USA, Dennison
late 1920s
Envelope measures 5.5"H x 8.5"W and contains a variety of items strung together on medium-weight orange string.
(1) **$375**
Because of their great rarity today, I suspect this experiment with small garlands was not successful.

▲ **String-Em-Outs**
USA, Dennison
late 1920s
Envelope measures 4"H x 12.5"W and contains 27 connected JOLs
(1) **$350**
Because of their great rarity today, I suspect this experiment with small garlands was not successful.

▲ **3-D black cat with scarf corner decoration**
USA, Beistle, (HE Luhrs mark)
1940s
21"H x 5"W x 12"L
(2) **$170**
The front legs pull away from the back legs, allowing the item to stand and providing a simple 3-D effect.

Shakers
Germany
8.75"H x 1.5"W x 4" diameter
The ubiquity of the imagery used here keeps the values low even though the shakers are very well made. They consist of paper reinforced with fiber pulled tautly over a cardboard frame with encircling thin wooden borders. There are metal bells attached along the rim to increase the noise level.
Left: 1920s, (3) **$135**
Right: 1930s, (4) **$115**

Shakers
Germany, 1920s
9"H x 1.25"W x 3.5" diameter
(2) **$195 each**
These unique noisemakers were made from thin paper over cardboard with red wooden handles.

Shaker with horn handle and bells
Germany, 1930s
10.25"H x 1.5"W x 4.75" diameter
(2) **$175**

Shaker with horn handle and bells
Germany, 1930s, 12.75"H x 1.5"W x 6.25" diameter, (2) **$225**
This is the largest shaker in this genre. Both the size and the very ornate design make this rare and desirable.

139

Paper over cardboard black cat face horn with wood top
USA, 1930s, 7"H
(2) **$95**

Paper over cardboard dancing JOL-people horn with wood top
USA, patented December 13, 1921
7.25"H, (3) **$75**

Paper over cardboard horns with identical imagery.
Left: USA, patented December 13, 1921
5.75"H, (3) **$75**
Right: Canada, Granger Company of Montreal, 1950s, 7.5"H, (2) **$150**

Paper over cardboard JOL and ivy horn with wood top
Germany
pre-1920s
21.5"H
(2) **$175**
This was one of the tallest cardboard horns made.

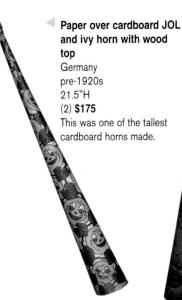

Paper over cardboard Screech Owl Siren Horn with metal top
USA, 1930s, 6.75"H, (3) **$75**
This horn not only has great graphics but makes an unusual sound. The cardboard bodies of this genre of horn were quite often re-used spindles from textile factories. Their labels will be often found affixed to the interiors.

Left: **Fairy scene horn with a gold foil cardboard top**
USA, Beistle, (no mark), 1920s, 9.5"H, (3) **$65**
This is made from one piece of heavy rolled cardboard.
Middle: **Cylindrical slider cardboard noisemaker**
USA, Bugle Toy Company, 1930s
10"H (closed) x 1.25" diameter, (4) **$65**
Right: **Paper over cardboard horn with gold foil top**
USA, Bugle Toy Company, 1930s, 7"H, (4) **$45**

Paper over cardboard horn
USA, Dennison
1930s
6.75"H
(4) **$45**

Paper over cardboard horn
USA, Dennison
1930s
6.75"H
(4) **$45**

Paper over cardboard horn
USA, Dennison
1930s
6.75"H
(4) **$55**
This horn has an unusually wide top opening.

Foil wrap over cardboard arched-back black cat horn
USA, Dennison
1930s
6.75"H
(4) **$40**

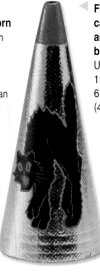

Paper over cardboard Veggie man horn with wood top
Germany
pre-1920s
12"H
(2) **$175**

Paper over cardboard devil horn with wood top
Germany
pre-1920s
14.25"H
(2) **$175**

Paper over cardboard multi-imaged horn with wood top
Germany
1920s
14.5"H
(2) **$135**

Paper over cardboard JOL and ivy horn with wood top
Germany
pre-1920s
13"H
(2) **$95**

Paper over cardboard horn
USA
late 1940s
6.75"H
(3) **$60**

Fairy scene horn with wood top
USA, Beistle, (no mark)
1920s
14.75"H
(2) **$120**
Made from one piece of heavy rolled cardboard, this was one of the tallest non-tin horns manufactured in the USA.

Paper over cardboard horns with wood tops
USA, Marks Brothers Company of Boston, Massachusetts
patented September 13, 1921
Left: 7.25"H
(2) **$105**
Middle: 15"H
(4) **$60**
Right: 7"H
(5) **$40**

Left: **Paper over cardboard horn with wood top**
USA, Bugle Toy Company
1930s
7"H
(4) **$45**
Right: **Paper over cardboard horn with gold foil cardboard top**
USA, Bugle Toy Company
1930s
7.25"H
(4) **$45**

Paper over cardboard Siren Horns with wood tops
USA, Marks Brothers Company of Boston, Massachusetts
1930s
6.75" to 7"H
(3) **$60 each**

NOISEMAKERS

141

Set of tin clickers
USA, US Metal Toy,
1940s, 2.5"H
From Left: (4) **$30**
(3) **$35**
(5) **$15**
(5) **$15**
(4) **$20**

Set of tin clickers
USA, Kirchhof (except
far right clicker by US
Metal Toy)
1950s
4.25"H
(5) **$20 each**

Tin clickers
USA, Kirchhof, "Life of the Party," 1950s, 3"H, (4) **$25 each**

Tin clickers
USA, T. Cohn, 1940s, 3" to 4"H, (5) **$20 each**

Scrap tin clickers
USA, Kirchhof
1950s
1.75"H
(3) **$45 each**
These are great examples of how the manufacturers
wrung every efficiency from their operations. Scrap
pieces left at the end of a shift would be made into
clickers. Because they were imperfect to begin with,
they would be sold locally at a discount. Today, true
scrap clickers are hard to come by and command a
small premium among collectors.

NOISEMAKERS

Tin shakers
USA, 1930s,
Top: 2.25"H, (2) **$75**
Bottom Left: 2.75"H, (3) **$50**
Bottom Right: 2.75"H, (3) **$65**
This is an unusual variant due to its black and
yellow body and its white ends.

Tin shakers
USA, US Metal Toy, 1930s.
Left: 3.25"H, (4) **$30**
Right: 3"H, (3) **$75**
This is an unusual variant due
to its tin horn handle.

Tin shaker
USA, J. Chein, (no mark)
1920s
3.25"H
(4) **$35**

Tin clickers.
Left: Japan, 1930s, 2.25"H, (2) **$95**
Right: Japan, 1950s, 3.25"H, (2) **$100**

Tin shaker
unknown
1930s
4.5"H
(3) **$110**

Ratchet and Shaker
Left: **Tin ratchet with open ends**
USA, Kirchhof, 1940s, 4"H, (4) **$25**
Right: **Tin shaker**
USA, Kirchhof, "Life of the Party,"1950s, 3.5"H, (5) **$20**

Tin shaker
USA, T. Cohn
1940s
3.25"H
(5) **$25**

**Tin ratchet with
open ends**
unknown
1920s
3.75"H
(3) **$50**

Tin shaker
USA, US Metal Toy
1960s
3.25"H
(5) **$20**

Tin shaker
USA, T. Cohn
early 1950s
3.25"H
(4) **$25**

Scrap tin clanger
USA, Kirchhof
1940s
3.75" diameter
(3) **$75**

Tin rattlers with wood handles
Left: USA, US Metal Toy, 1920s, 4" diameter, (4) **$50**
Middle: USA, Kirchhof, 1920s, 4.5" diameter, (3) **$75**
Right: USA, (probably Bugle Toy), 1920s, 4" diameter, (3) **$95**

Tin rattlers with wood handles
Left: USA, 1920s, 3.25" diameter, (3) **$40**
Right: USA, T. Cohn, 1930s, 3.5" diameter, (3) **$35**

Tin rattlers with wood handles
USA, US Metal Toy, 1920s, 3" diameter
(3) **$35 each**

Tin rattlers
USA, Kirchhof, 1930s, 3" diameter
Left: (4) **$35**
Middle: (3) **$50**
Right: (4) **$45**

Tin rattlers with wood handles
USA, Kirchhof, "Life of the Party"
1950s, 3.25" diameter
(5) **$20 each**

Tin rattlers with wood handles
USA, T. Cohn
3.25" diameter
Left: 1940s, (5) **$35**
Right: 1940s, (4) **$40**

NOISEMAKERS

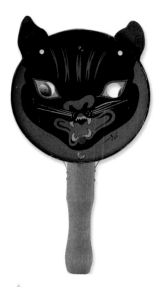

Tin bell
USA
1920s
6"H x 3"W
(4) **$75**

Tin siren noisemaker
USA
1950s
3.5"H x 2.25"W
(4) **$65**

Tin clanger
USA, T. Cohn
1920s
8.25"H x 4" diameter
(1) **$175**
This highly unusual noisemaker
has attached wood balls
painted like eyes, as well as the
original cardboard ears, giving
it a truly finished look. This is
one of the earliest and most
rare T. Cohn items in this
collection.

Tin clangers
3.75" diameter.
Left: USA, Kirchhof, 1940s, (5) **$25**
Middle: USA, Kirchhof, "Life of the Party," 1950s, (5) **$20**
Right: USA, US Metal Toy, 1920s, (4) **$25**

Tin rattlers with wood handles
3.25" diameter.
Left: USA, US Metal Toy, 1950s, (5) **$15**
Right: T. Cohn, 1950s, (4) **$20**

Tin shaker
USA, Kirchhof
1940s
6.75"H x 4" diameter
(4) **$25**

Tin dual-sided clapper
USA
1920s
8"H x 3.25" diameter
(2) **$225**

NOISEMAKERS

Tin "putty knife" clanger
USA, T. Cohn, 1940s, 7"H x 2.5"W, (3) **$60**

Tin "putty knife" clanger
USA, T. Cohn, 1940s, 7"H x 2.5"W, (2) **$70**

Dual-sided tin shakers with horn handles
USA, T. Cohn, 1920s, 11.75"H x 4" diameter, (2) **$175 each**

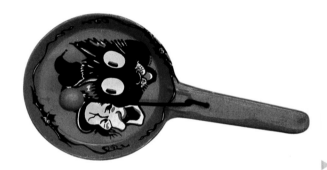

Tin horn
USA, Kirchhof
1920s
5.5"H
(2) **$125**
This item, clearly using Dennison artwork, also has a "Made in Japan" counterpart, which has a lesser value.

Tin pan clanger
USA, Bugle Toy
1920s
7.75"H x 4" diameter
(2) **$75**

Tin slider
USA, Kirchhof
1920s
10"L (closed)
(4) **$85**

Assortment of noisemakers
USA, Bugle Toy
1920s
From Left:
Ratchet, 4.75"H
(3) **$55**
Clicker, 3"H
(3) **$50**
Ratchet, 4.75"H
(2) **$100**
Clanger, 3.75" diameter
(3) **$70**
Rectangular Shaker, 4"L
(2) **$90**
Shaker, 3.75" diameter
(2) **$100**

◀ **Tin three-sided ratchet**
Germany
1920s
4.75"H
(2) **$90**

◀ **Tin ratchet**
USA
|US Metal Toy
1940s
4.25"H
(4) **$20**

◀ **Tin three-sided ratchet**
USA
Kirchhof, 1930s,
4.75"H
(3) **$50**

▶ **Tin ratchets**
USA, T. Cohn
1930s
4.5"H
(4) **$30 each**

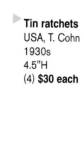

▼ **Tin ratchets**
USA, Kirchhof
Left: 6.25"H, (2) **$100**
This item has a patent date of
November 27, 1928.
Right: 1950s, 4.5"H, (5) **$15**

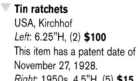

▲ **Tin ratchets**.
Left: USA, Kirchhof, "Life of the Party," 1950s, 4.5"H, (5) **$15**
Right: USA, T. Cohn, 1940s, 4" diameter, (4) **$25**

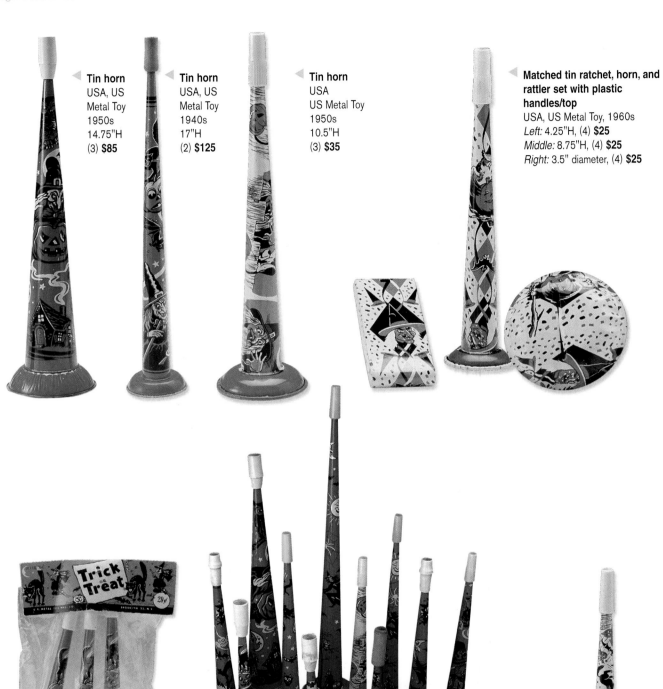

◄ **Tin horn**
USA, US
Metal Toy
1950s
14.75"H
(3) **$85**

◄ **Tin horn**
USA, US
Metal Toy
1940s
17"H
(2) **$125**

◄ **Tin horn**
USA
US Metal Toy
1950s
10.5"H
(3) **$35**

◄ **Matched tin ratchet, horn, and rattler set with plastic handles/top**
USA, US Metal Toy, 1960s
Left: 4.25"H, (4) **$25**
Middle: 8.75"H, (4) **$25**
Right: 3.5" diameter, (4) **$25**

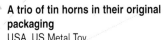

▲ **A trio of tin horns in their original packaging**
USA, US Metal Toy
1950s
9.75"H x 6"W
(3) **$75**

▲ **Assortment of tin horns of varying manufacturers**
USA, Kirchhof
1940s–1950s
The tallest horn is 18" (the largest one made).
(3) **$125**

▲ **Matched tin ratchet and horn set with plastic handle/top**
USA, 1960s, 4.5" to 9"H
(4) **$25 each**

NOISEMAKERS

Complete set of diamond patterned noisemakers
USA, 1960s, all handles are plastic.
From Left:
Round Ratchet
3.5" diameter, (5) **$10**
Rectangular Ratchet
4.75"H, (5) **$10**
Oblong Ratchet
4.75"H, (5) **$10**
Clanger
7.25"H x 3"W, (2) **$50**
Tambourine
6.25" diameter, (2) **$225**
Shaker
3.25" diameter, (5) **$10**

Oblong tin ratchets.
From Left: USA, T. Cohn, 1940s, 5.25"H, (4) **$25**
USA, US Metal Toy, 5.25"H, 1950s, (5) **$15**
USA, T. Cohn 1940s, 5.25"H, (4) **$30**
USA, T. Cohn, 1950s, 5.25"H, (5) **$20**

Oblong tin ratchet
USA, T. Cohn
1950s
5.25"H
(5) **$25**

Tin ratchet
USA, J. Chein, (no mark)
1920s
4" diameter
(2), **$175**.

Tin ratchet
USA, Kirchhof
1920s
4" diameter
(2) **$245**

Tin ratchet
USA, J. Chein, (no mark)
1920s
4" diameter
(4) **$35**

NOISEMAKERS

149

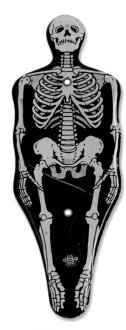

Left: **Tin sparkler**
USA, 1920s, 5"H x 2.75" diameter, (3) **$75**
Right: **Tin pan clanger**
USA, J. Chein, (no mark), 1920s
6.5"H x 2.75" diameter
(3) **$100**

Tin skeleton shaker with plastic handle
USA, US Metal Toy, 1960s,
8"H x 2.75"W, (3) **$70**

Tin witch ratchet with plastic handle
USA, US Metal Toy, 1960s, 4.75"H x 4.25"W, (4) **$65**

Tin ratchets
USA, 4" diameter
Left: T. Cohn, 1930s
(4) **$25**
Middle: Kirchhof, 1940s
(5) **$25**
Right: T. Cohn, 1950s
(5) **$25**

Tin ratchets
USA, US Metal Toy
Left: 1950s, 4" diameter, (5) **$20**
Right: 1940s, 4" diameter, (4) **$25**

Tin ratchets
USA, T. Cohn
1930s, 4" diameter
(4) **$25 each**

Tin pan clanger
USA, J. Chein,
(circular mark)
1920s
8"H x 4" diameter
(2) **$100**

Tin pan clanger with wood siren horn handle
USA, T. Cohn
1920s
9.25"H x 4" diameter
(3) **$55**

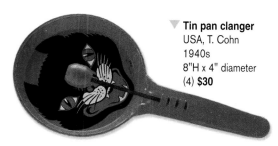

Tin pan clanger
USA, T. Cohn
1940s
8"H x 4" diameter
(4) **$30**

Tin convex clanger
USA, T. Cohn
1930s
8.5"H x 4.25" diameter
(3) **$40**

Tin pan clanger
USA, Kirchhof, 1940s
8.5"H x 3.25"W
(3) **$45**

Tin sparkler with original box
USA, J. Chein, 1920s
5"H x 1.75"W x 2.25"L
Sparkler: (3) **$150**
Box: The box has two patent numbers with the higher one being 1,558,450.
(2) **$125**

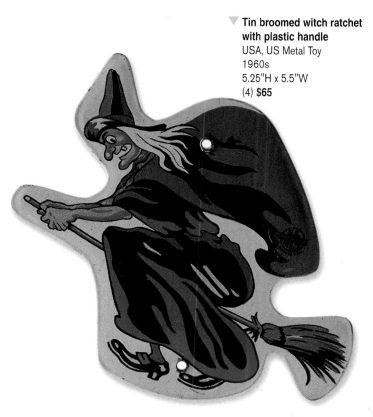

Tin broomed witch ratchet with plastic handle
USA, US Metal Toy
1960s
5.25"H x 5.5"W
(4) **$65**

▶ **Tin convex clangers**
USA, Kirchhof, "Life of the Party"
8.5"H x 4.5" diameter
Left: 1960s, (5) **$20**
Note how the manufacturer replaced the wood balls with cheaper tin clangers to increase the profit margin.
Right: 1950s, (4) **$30**

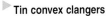

▶ **Tin convex clangers**
Left: USA, Kirchhof, "Life of the Party," 1950s
8.5"H x 4.5" diameter, (5) **$25**
Right: USA, T. Cohn, 1930s
8.25"H x 4.25" diameter, (3) **$50**
This item is identically dual-sided.

▶ **Tin pan clangers**
USA, T. Cohn, 8"H x 4" diameter
Left: 1940s, (4) **$30**
Right: 1930s, (3) **$35**

▶ **Tin clangers**
USA, T. Cohn
1930s
Left: **Pan clanger**
8"H x 4" diameter
(4) **$30**
Right: **Convex clanger**
8.25"H x 4" diameter
(3) **$35**

▶ **Tin clangers**
USA, J. Chein
8"H x 4.25" diameter
Left: **Pan clanger**
1920s
(circular mark)
(3) **$90**
Right: **Convex clanger**
1920s
(no mark)
(3) **$90**

Tin pan clanger
USA, Kirchhof
1930s
6.5"H x 2.75"W
(2) **$65**

Clanger
USA, J. Chein, 1930s, 10"H x 6.25"W, (2) **$150**
The imagery seen on this clanger is common, but
what is not is this form. This clanger is made from
taut paper decorated on both sides stretched
tightly to a tin frame.

Tin pan clanger
USA, US Metal Toy
1960s
7.25"H x 3"W
(3) **$35**

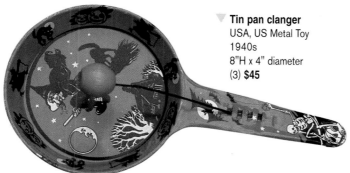

Tin pan clanger
USA, US Metal Toy
1940s
8"H x 4" diameter
(3) **$45**

Skull squeaker
Germany, pre-1920s, 2.5" diameter, (2) **$150**

**Identically-sided cardboard
cat accordion squeaker**
Germany, 1920s, 5.75"H x 3.5"L
(2) **$250**

Cardboard cat squeakers
unknown, 1930s
Left: 5.5"H x 2.75"L, (3) **$165**
Right: 5.5"H x 2.5"L, (2) **$165**

**Identically-sided cardboard witch
squeaker**
unknown, 1920s, 5.5"H x 4.25"L
(2) **$250**

NOISEMAKERS

Wooden horn
Czechoslovakia
1920s
6"H
(2) **$70**

Wooden horn
Czechoslovakia
1920s
5.75"H
(2) **$90**

Tin clicker
Germany
1930s
3.75"H
(3) **$65**

Identically-sided cardboard owl accordion squeaker with tin handles
Japan
1930s
4.75"H x 3.75"L
(2) **$150**

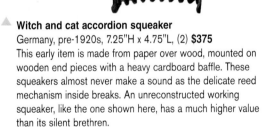

Witch and cat accordion squeaker
Germany, pre-1920s, 7.25"H x 4.75"L, (2) **$375**
This early item is made from paper over wood, mounted on wooden end pieces with a heavy cardboard baffle. These squeakers almost never make a sound as the delicate reed mechanism inside breaks. An unreconstructed working squeaker, like the one shown here, has a much higher value than its silent brethren.

Set of tin clickers
Germany
1930s
1.75" to 2"H
(3) **$40 each**

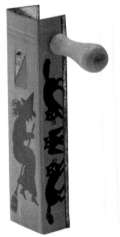

Tin ratchets
Germany
1930s
4.75"H
Left: (3) **$110**
Right: (3) **$125**

Clanger with horn handle
Czechoslovakia, 1920s, 11.5"H x 4.25"
diameter, (2) **$225**
This paper over cardboard item with a wood
handle has a full-bodied black cat image on the
reverse side. Czech items overall are rare.

Identically-sided cardboard cat face shaker
USA, C.A. Reed Company of Williamsport, Pennsylvania
1940s, 8.25"H x 1.5"W x 3"L, (3) **$45**

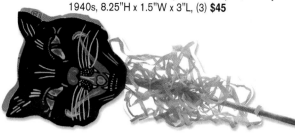

Tin ratchet
Germany
1930s
6.75"H x 4.5" diameter
(2) **$160**

Tin clanger
Germany
1930s
8.75"H x 4.5" diameter
(3) **$125**

Tin clangers
Germany
1930s
8.75"H x 4.5" diameter
(3) **$125 each**

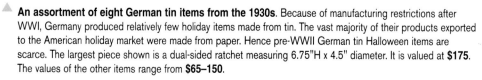

An assortment of eight German tin items from the 1930s. Because of manufacturing restrictions after
WWI, Germany produced relatively few holiday items made from tin. The vast majority of their products exported
to the American holiday market were made from paper. Hence pre-WWII German tin Halloween items are
scarce. The largest piece shown is a dual-sided ratchet measuring 6.75"H x 4.5" diameter. It is valued at **$175**.
The values of the other items range from **$65–150**.

Tin sparkler
Germany
1930s
4.5"H x 1.75" diameter
(3) **$125**

Tin tambourine with a paper face
USA, T. Cohn, 1930s, 6.5" diameter
(4) **$40**

Tin tambourine with reinforced-paper face
USA, Ohio Art Company of Bryan, Ohio,
1940s, 6.25" diameter, (4) **$50**
The artwork was done by Fern Bisel Peat, a
prominent illustrator.

Tin tambourine with a reinforced-paper face
USA, 1940s, 9" diameter, (4) **$50**

Tambourine
Germany, 1930s, 6.5" diameter
(4) **$100**
Although fragile (consisting of taut paper over a wood
frame), these were made in very great quantities.

Hard plastic tambourine
USA, Lapin Company of Newark, New Jersey, 1950s,
6" diameter, (3) **$100**
This orange/black creation has a party scene on the
black face in raised relief. The variant with the orange
face is much more rare and has a significantly higher
value.

Tin tambourine
unknown, 1920s, 6.25" diameter, (2) **$275**
Although this is one of the most rare of tin tambourines,
the value doesn't reflect this, probably due to the
primitive and minimalist imagery.

Tin tambourine
USA, 1930s, 6.25" diameter, (3) **$175**
The artwork along the rim is very similar to the imagery
on several Kirchhof horns, so there is a strong
probability this was made by Kirchhof.

NOISEMAKERS

Tambourine
Germany, 1930s, 6.5" diameter
(3) **$165**

Tin tambourine with decorated rim
USA, J. Chein, (circular mark), 1920s, 7" diameter
(3) **$250**

Tin tambourine
unknown, 1930s, 6.25" diameter
(2) **$300**

Tin tambourine with decorated rim
USA, J. Chein, (circular mark), 1920s, 7" diameter
(4) **$250.** In later iterations, the goose's eye is missing.

Tin tambourine with decorated rim
USA, J. Chein, (circular mark), 1920s, 7" diameter
(2) **$325**

Tin tambourine with decorated rim
USA, J. Chein, (circular mark), 1920s, 7" diameter
(3) **$250**

157

▲ **Tin tambourines.**
Left: USA, Kirchhof, 1930s, 6.25" diameter, (4) **$85**
Right: USA, (probably Kirchhof due to the use of Dennison imagery)
1940s, 6.25" diameter, (4) **$75**

▲ **Tin tambourines**
1940s
Left: USA, (probably Kirchhof due to the use of Dennison imagery)
6.25" diameter, (5) **$70**
Right: USA, (probably Kirchhof due to the use of Dennison imagery)
6.25" diameter, (3) **$150**

▲ **Tin tambourine with decorated rim**
USA, J. Chein, (circular mark), 1920s, 7" diameter, (2) **$325**

▲ **Tin tambourines**
USA, T. Cohn, 1950s, 7.25" diameter, (5) **$60 each**

▲ **Tin tambourine with decorated rim**
USA, J. Chein, (shield mark), 1930s, 7" diameter, (3) **$225**

▲ **Tin tambourines**
USA, Kirchhof, "Life of the Party," 1950s, 6.25" diameter, (5) **$75 each**

▲ **Tin tambourine with decorated rim**
USA, J. Chein, (shield mark), 1930s, 7" diameter, (4) **$225**

▲ **Printed paper-faced tambourine with decorated tin rim**
USA, 1930s, 7" diameter, (2) **$225**

▲ **Tin tambourine**
USA, 1960s, 6.25" diameter, (2) **$225**

▲ **Tin tambourine**
USA, T. Cohn, 1930s, 6.25" diameter, (1) **$450**

▲ **Tin tambourine**
USA, 1930s, 6.25" diameter, (2) **$250**

◀ **Tin items**
USA
1920s
Ends: **Cymbals**
5.5" diameter
(1), **$475 set**.
Middle: **Gotham Rattler**
5.5"H x 4" diameter
(3) **$55**

DIECUTS

The word diecuts encompasses the genre of either flat or embossed paper goods that would be generally hung on walls to lend a festive air to the Halloween party. Most of the products made in the United States were flat or perhaps had a slight bit of embossing. Most of the items made in Germany were heavily embossed and had painted highlights applied by hand, giving these pieces a true dimensionality and personality unlike any others. Some German diecuts were glazed; most were not. Although the glazed pieces seem to have held up better over time, there is no difference in value between glazed or unglazed items, all else being equal.

The 12 different German tiaras are a fun exception to the wall-clinging nature of most diecuts. They are also a great example of a good idea tripped up by the real world. Made to wrap around the front of a person's head, and held in place by thin black elastic string, these elegantly designed items were beautiful to look at, but impractical, as they bent and continually slipped off. Even the most common of these tiaras were made for only a few years, with the more rare versions made for a single season only. Because of their intended use, it is quite difficult to find these today in collectible condition.

Reproductions haven't been much of an issue. Manufacturers have re-issued diecuts using original plates but greatly varying the colors, making it easy to differentiate new from old. Most of the modern versions are also double-sided, whereas the vintage versions are almost always single-sided. Christopher Radko has released a line of diecuts based on the original German designs. His versions differ in size, colors used, by the application of glitter, and by their flat backs making these impossible to confuse with vintage diecuts.

◀ **Party Signs**
USA
(probably Whitney)
1930s
7.75"H x 14.25"W
non-embossed
(2) **$80 each**

▶ **Hallowe'en Silhouettes Jointed Bat and Hoot Owl envelope with diecuts**
USA, Beistle
(no mark)
early 1920s
Envelope: 11.25"H x 6.75"W, (2) **$80**
Bat: 9"H x 9.75"W, non-embossed, (2) **$135**
Hoot Owl: 9"H x 11.5"W, non-embossed, (2) **$145**

▶ **Door hanger**
USA, Dennison
appeared in their
1928 Party Magazine
9.5"H x 4.75"W
non-embossed
(4) **$45**

▲ **Witch and Cat Decorations envelopes
(fronts and back)**
USA, Beistle
(stated on envelope)
1920s
Each envelope contains four black/orange non-embossed diecuts: two large and two small versions of the imagery on the envelopes, each marked, "Made in USA."
Envelopes: 13.25"H x 10.5"W, (2) **$125 each**
Large witch: 11"H x 9.5"W, (3) **$40**
Small witch: 4.25"H x 3.75"W, (3) **$20**
Large cat: 10.25"H x 8.5"W, (3) **$40**
Small cat: 4.5"H x 3.5"W, (3) **$20**

▼ **Door hangers**
USA, Dennison
Left: early 1930s, 9"H x 7.5"W, non-embossed, (3) **$75**
Middle: appeared in their 1928 Party Magazine
9.75"H x 4.5"W, non-embossed, (4) **$45**
Right: appeared in their 1930 Price List pamphlet
10"H x 7.75"W, non-embossed, (3) **$70**

◄ **Set of seven small diecuts**
USA, Beistle, (no mark)
late 1930s
lightly embossed
Smoking JOL:
5.75"H x 4.25"W, (3) **$35**
Clown:
5.75"H x 4"W, (3) **$20**
Witch face:
6.25"H x 4"W, (2) **$50**
Skull with cap:
5.75"H x 4.25"W, (3) **$25**
Pirate cat:
5.25"H x 4"W, (3) **$25**
Cat with bells:
6"H x 4"W, (3) **$30**
JOL witch face:
6"H x 4"W, (2) **$45**

▲ **Complete set of four small diecuts**
USA, (probably Whitney)
1930s
4" to 5"H x 3.75" to 4"W
non-embossed
(2) **$55 set**

◄ **Complete set of four small diecuts**
USA
1930s
5.25" to 7"H x 4.5" to 5.5"W
non-embossed
(3) **$45 set**

▶ **Set of 4 diecuts**
USA, Beistle, (no mark)
late 1930s
lightly embossed
Upper Left: 6"H x 8.75"W
(3) **$55**
Upper Right: 6"H x 8.5"W
(2) **$95**
Lower Left: 6"H x 8.5"W
(2) **$90**
Lower Right: 5.75"H x 8.75"W
(3) **$65**

▼ Pumpkin garland
USA, Beistle
(no mark)
pre-1920s
65"L
non-embossed
(1) **$275**

**▲ Complete set of three
pirate themed diecuts**
USA, Beistle, (no mark)
1950s
17.25" to 17.75"H x 6.25"
to 6.75"W
lightly embossed
(5) **$25 each**

▶ Crow
USA, Dennison
appeared in their
1928 Party Magazine
9"H x 5"W
non-embossed
(3) **$45**

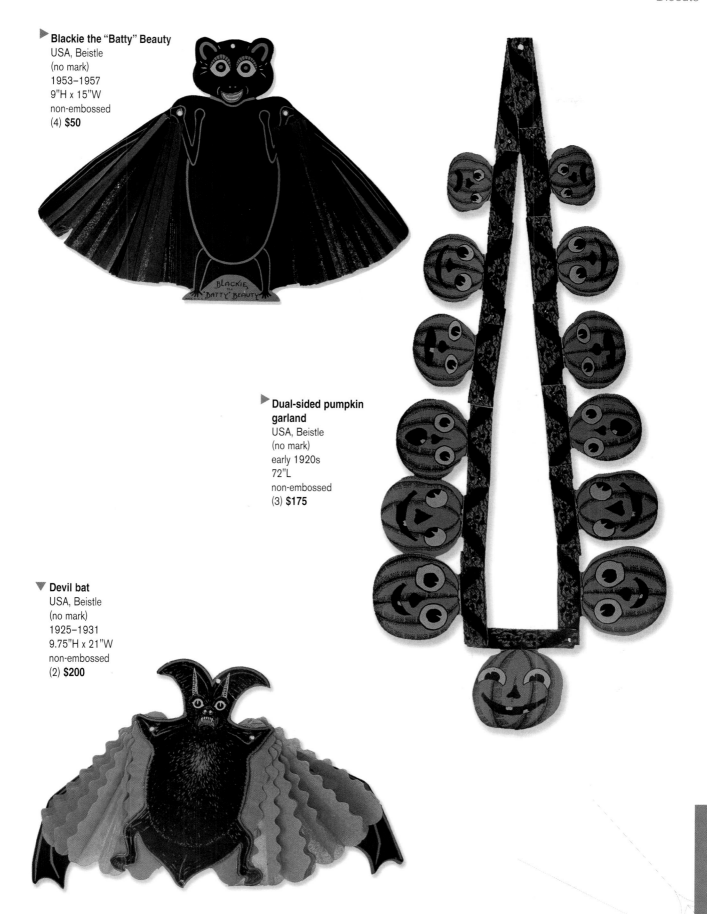

Blackie the "Batty" Beauty
USA, Beistle
(no mark)
1953–1957
9"H x 15"W
non-embossed
(4) **$50**

Dual-sided pumpkin garland
USA, Beistle
(no mark)
early 1920s
72"L
non-embossed
(3) **$175**

Devil bat
USA, Beistle
(no mark)
1925–1931
9.75"H x 21"W
non-embossed
(2) **$200**

This complete set of 12 diecuts (plus the separate duo set of the witch and pirate faces) was made by Beistle off and on from 1932 through the late 1940s. Some pieces seem to have been made more than others, which is reflected in the rarity index number assigned to each. It is difficult to determine when a particular piece was made, as the manufacturer was quite consistent with both colors and markings throughout the entire run. One clue, however, is the embossing. Earlier iterations have a deeper, more refined embossing than later iterations, which tend to be nearly flat. Additionally, earlier iterations will often have the words "Made in USA" embossed somewhere on the piece. These clues can help roughly date a piece, which is important as the older iterations tend to have a greater value. Each diecut measures 9.25" to 9.5"H x 8.25" to 8.5"W.

▶ These unusual color variations were made for perhaps a single season in the very early 1930s.
Left: 9.25"H x 8.25"W
(2) **$65**
Right: 9.25"H x 8.25"W
(2) **$80**

▶ *Left:* (3) **$50**
Right: (4) **$30**

▶ *Left:* (4) **$25**
Right: (4) **$40**

▶ *Left:* (3) **$55**
Right: (4) **$30**

DIECUTS

Left: (3) **$55**
Right: (4) **$30**

Left: (4) **$40**
Right: (4) **$40**

Left: (3) **$60**
Right: (3) **$85**

Some iterations of these
diecuts were made with easels.
Left: 12"H x 12"W
(4) **$40**
Right: 12"H x 12"W
(4) **$55**

Hobo clown with JOL
USA
1920s
8.25"H x 5.5"W
non-embossed
(2) **$35**

Clown with JOL
USA
1920s
8"H x 5.75"W
non-embossed
(2) **$45**

Whoopee in a tub
USA, Dennison
1920s
15"H x 11.5"W
non-embossed
(1) **$300**

JOL-headed traffic cop
USA, Dennison
appeared in their 1930
Price List pamphlet
13.25"H x 12.25"W
non-embossed
(2) **$200**

Cat and witch singing
USA, Dennison
appeared in their
1928 Party Magazine
15.75"H x 12"W
non-embossed
(2) **$165**

Surprised moon with owls
USA, Dennison
appeared in their
1929 Party Magazine
12.5" diameter
non-embossed
(2) **$145**
The prominent use of gray is
unusual. The imagery looks similar to
the moon logo later used by Jackie
Gleason on his television show.

Jointed scarecrow
USA, Beistle
(no mark)
1950s
37"H
non-embossed
(3) **$75**

**Jointed Spooky Spider in
original package**
USA, Beistle
("A Beistle Creation" mark)
early 1960s
24"H x 32"W
non-embossed
(3) **$125**

169

▶ **"Eats" sign**
USA, Dennison
appeared in their 1930
Price List pamphlet
11.5"H x 14"W
non-embossed
(2) **$150**

▶ **Witch face**
USA, Dennison
appeared in their 1930
Price List pamphlet
12"H x 10.5"W
non-embossed
(3) **$75**

▶ **Broomed witch against moon**
USA, Beistle
(no mark)
early 1930s
18.5"H x 12"W
heavily embossed
(3) **$125**
This item is superbly
designed with scalloped
edges and great
detailing. The steeple's
clock reads 12:05! Most
of these came with
easels.

**Ferocious witch face
with crepe hair**
USA, Beistle
(no mark)
1940–1960s
18.25"H x 14.25"W
non-embossed
(4) **$60**
This was sometimes
marketed as "Creepy Alice."

**Broomed witch against
yellow moon**
USA
1960s
12.5"H x 18.5"W
non-embossed
(2) **$50**
This diecut was re-issued
in the late 1960s with two
identical sides. That
iteration has a lesser value.

Witch face with mice
USA, Beistle
(no mark)
late 1940s
17.75"H x 12"W
lightly embossed
(5) **$35**

**Witch face with
transparency**
USA, Beistle
(no mark)
late 1940s
8.5"H x 6"W
non-embossed
(3) **$60**

◄ **Tri-fold "Spookie Shade" fireplace screen**
USA
has a patent date of August 1907
9.75"H x 12"W
non-embossed
(1) **$200**

◄ **Witch by cauldron**
USA, Beistle
(no mark)
late 1940s
17.25"H x 6.25"W
lightly embossed
(5) **$25**

◄ **Tri-fold "Spookie Shade" fireplace screen**
USA
has a patent date of August 1907
15"H x 15.5"W
non-embossed
(1) **$700**

◄ **"This Way" owl sign**
USA, Dennison
appears in their
1928 Party Magazine
8.5"H x 15"W
non-embossed
(3) **$65**

Owl
USA, Dennison
appeared in their 1920
Bogie Book
18"H x 10.5"W
non-embossed
(2) **$70**

Left: **Owl**
USA, Dennison
early 1920s
8.75"H x 5.25"W
non-embossed, (2) **$35**
Right: **Cat**
USA, Dennison
early 1920s
8.5"H x 6.25"W
non-embossed
(2) **$35**

Owl
USA
The Gibson Art
Company of
Cincinnati, Ohio
1930s
9.5"H x 9"W
non-embossed
(2) **$45**

"Wise Up!" owl
USA
The Gibson Art
Company of
Cincinnati, Ohio
1930s
13.5"H x 7"W
non-embossed
(2) **$85**

◀ **Owl against moon with leaves at bottom**
USA, Beistle
(no mark)
early 1930s
18.5"H x 12"W
heavily embossed
(3) **$75**

▲ **JOL**
USA, Dennison
1920s
8.25"H x 9.75"W
non-embossed
(3) **$30**

◀ **Owl holding "This Way" sign**
USA, Beistle
(printed name)
appears in their 1948 catalog
11.25"H x 10.5"W
non-embossed
(4) **$45**

▲ **JOL**
USA
Dennison, appeared in their 1935
Hallowe'en Parties magazine
9"H x 11.25"W
non-embossed
(3) **$30**

▲ **JOL**
USA, Beistle, (HE Luhrs mark)
1940s, 6"H x 8.5"W
lightly embossed
(2) **$45**

▲ *Left:* **Green and orange JOL**
USA, Beistle, (no mark), 1932–late 1940s
12" diameter, heavily embossed, (4) **$50**
Right: **Cat atop JOL**
USA, Beistle, (no mark), 1932–late 1940s
12" diameter, heavily embossed, (4) **$50**

◄ **JOLs**
USA, Beistle
(HE Luhrs mark)
1940s
6.25"H x 8.5"W
lightly embossed
(2) **$45 each**

▼ **JOL with cap**
USA, (probably Beistle)
early 1950s
10"H x 8.25"W
non-embossed
(2) **$60**
This has an attached
fold-out section on the
back that gives the piece
great dimensionality.

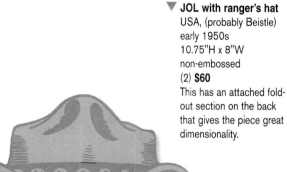

▼ **JOL with ranger's hat**
USA, (probably Beistle)
early 1950s
10.75"H x 8"W
non-embossed
(2) **$60**
This has an attached fold-
out section on the back
that gives the piece great
dimensionality.

▲ **JOL with top hat**
USA
(probably Beistle)
early 1950s
10.75"H x 8.25"W
non-embossed
(2) **$60**
This has an attached
fold-out section on the
back that gives the
piece great
dimensionality.

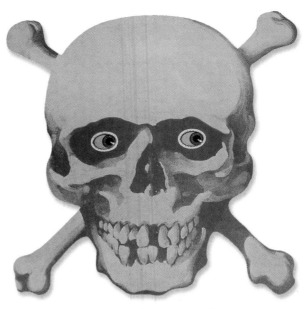

▲ **Skull and crossbones**
USA, Dennison
appeared in their 1933
Hallowe'en Book
9"H x 9"W
non-embossed
(2) **$165**

▶ **JOL with hat**
USA, Beistle
(printed name)
late 1940s
20.5"H x 14.25"W
non-embossed
(3) **$50**
This was made with
an unusually heavy
cardboard stock.

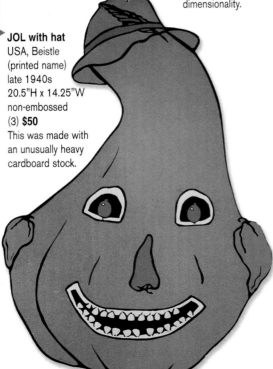

▲ **Skull and
crossbones with
separately attached
piece allowing the
eyes to move**
USA, Beistle
(no mark)
1950s
9.5"H x 8.25"W
slightly embossed
(4) **$35**

Jointed skeleton with original packaging
USA, Beistle
(HE Luhrs mark)
1940s
11.75"H x 6.75"W
non-embossed
Beistle assigned stock number 1646 to this item.
Skeleton
(5) **$10**
Advertising Card
(2) **$30**

Hallowe'en Skeleton envelope with contents
USA, Dennison
1920s
17"H x 13"W
(3) **$40**

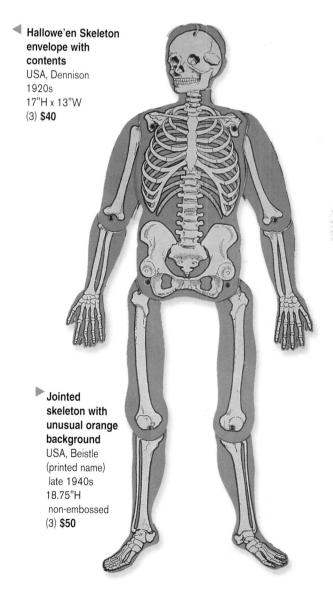

Pointing shrouded skeleton with sign
USA, The Gibson Art Company of Cincinnati, Ohio
1940s
11.25"H x 18"W
non-embossed
(2) **$150**
Due to a poor design, the hand is nearly always missing or detached.

Jointed skeleton with unusual orange background
USA, Beistle
(printed name)
late 1940s
18.75"H
non-embossed
(3) **$50**

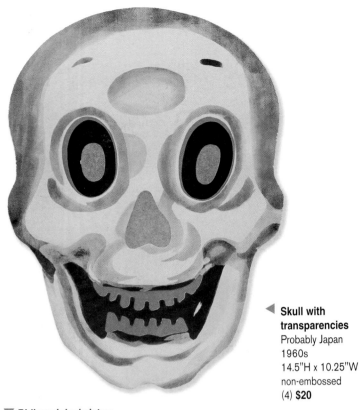

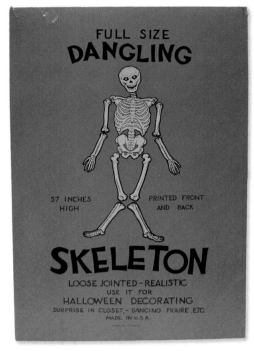

◀ **Skull with transparencies**
Probably Japan
1960s
14.5"H x 10.25"W
non-embossed
(4) **$20**

▲ **Dangling Skeleton envelope with contents**
USA, Beistle
(printed name)
copyrighted 1935
22"H x 15"W
(2) **$60**

▼ **Riding pink skeleton with JOL**
USA
1950s
15"H x 10.75"W
non-embossed
(2) **$85**

▶ **Hallowe'en skeleton envelope with contents**
USA, Beistle
(no mark)
1930s
22"H x 12"W
(3) **$55**

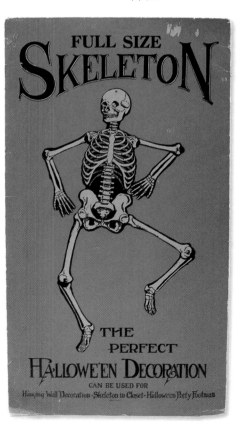

Snarling cat face
USA, Dennison
appeared in their 1928 Party
Magazine
11"H x 10"W
non-embossed
(3) **$40**
This diecut came in three sizes. The
smallest is 5.5"H x 5"W and the
largest is 17"H x 15.25"W.

Running skeleton with toothy grin
USA, Dennison
first appeared in their 1929 Parties
magazine
22"H x 20"W
non-embossed
(2) **$250**
These are rarely found intact. Because
the extremities extend beyond the main
borders they are nearly always truncated
or detached.

Jointed cat
USA, Beistle, (no mark)
1930s
21"H x 12.5"W
non-embossed
(2) **$125**
This variant with green
eyes and red mouth was
made only for a season
or two and is rarely seen.

Orange skull
USA, The Gibson Art
Company of
Cincinnati, Ohio
1940s
5"H x 4"W
non-embossed
(3) **$35**

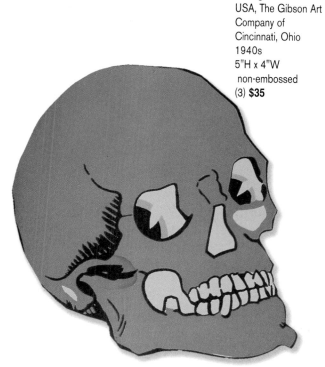

▼ **Jointed cat**
USA, Beistle
(no mark)
1950s
12.75"H x 14.25"W
non-embossed
(5) **$30**

▼ **Jointed cat**
USA, Beistle
(no mark)
1950s
8.5"H x 8"W
non-embossed
(5) **$20**

▶ **Jointed cat**
USA, Beistle
(Bee-Line mark)
1948–1952
9"H x 8"W
non-embossed
(4) **$20**

◀ **Jointed cat with
original advertising
band**
USA, Beistle
(no mark)
late 1920s
10"H x 12"W
non-embossed
(4) **$40**

– ONE –
HALLOWE'EN BLACK CAT
WITH
MOVABLE TAIL AND LEGS
SIZE 10 x 12 INCHES
No. 1624   MADE IN U.S.A.

Complete set of eight
black cat band members
USA, Beistle
(HE Luhrs mark)
1940s
8.75" to 9"H
lightly embossed.
From Left: (4) **$20**
(3) **$30**
(4) **$25**
(3) **$30**

From Left: (4) **$20**
(4) **$20**
(4) **$25**
(3) **$30**

Complete set of
four black cat band
members
USA, Beistle
(HE Luhrs mark)
1940s
17.5" to 18.5"H
lightly embossed
From Left: (3) **$55**
(4) **$45**
(4) **$45**
(4) **$45**

▼ **Arched-back black cat**
USA, Dennison
first appeared in their
1920 Bogie Book
18"H x 14.5"W
non-embossed
(2) $55

▼ **Art Deco cat face**
USA, Beistle
(no mark)
1930s
12"H x 12"W
lightly embossed
(4) $55

◄ **Cat with monocle**
Canada, Make-Believe Playsuits, Incorporated
1950
8.25"H x 6.25"W
non-embossed
(2) $120

This is a quite different from the *very* common cat with monocle
diecut issued for decades by Beistle.

▲ **Black cat face**
USA, Beistle
(no mark)
1930s
12"H x 12"W
lightly embossed
(4) $45

DIECUTS

Cat on a moon
USA, Dennison
pre-1920s
12"H x 10.5"W
non-embossed
(2) **$105**

**Mechanical
cat diecut**
USA
1920s
8.25"H x 5"W
non-embossed
(2) **$125**
As the tail is
moved, the eyes
change pupils.

**Cat against
yellow moon**
USA
1940s
13"H x 14.5"W
non-embossed
(1) **$150**

Jointed skelecat
USA, Beistle, (printed name)
1960s
16.25"H x 15"W
non-embossed
(3) **$125**

▼ **Jointed skelecat**
USA, Beistle
(printed name)
1960s
18.5"H x 15"W
non-embossed
(3) **$135**

◄ **Cat with devil mask**
USA, Beistle
(printed name)
1949–1953
13"H x 9"W
non-embossed
(3) **$110**

▼ *Top:* **JOL**
USA, Beistle, (HE Luhrs mark)
1940s–1950s, 9"H x 12"W
lightly embossed, (5) **$15**
Bottom Left: **Black cat face**
USA, Beistle
(HE Luhrs mark)
1940s–1950s
9.75"H x 12.5"W
lightly embossed
(5) **$15**
Bottom Right: **Black cat face**
USA, Beistle
(HE Luhrs mark)
1940s–1950s
9"H x 12"W
lightly embossed
(5) **$15**

▲ **Full-bodied black cat**
USA, Beistle
(no mark)
1930s
18.5"H x 12"W
heavily embossed
(3) **$75**
This item has an easel.

Cat walking along fence top
USA, Beistle
(printed name)
1949–1953
9.75"H x 22.5"W
non-embossed
(3) **$60**

Cat on fence top with moon behind
USA, Beistle
(printed name)
1949–1953
20"H x 12.5"W
non-embossed
(3) **$60**

Black cat faces
USA, Beistle, (HE Luhrs mark), 1940s
6"H x 8.5"W, lightly embossed, (3) **$30 each**

Left: **Jointed foil dressed cat with original wrap tag**
USA, 1950s, 13"H x 8"W, lightly embossed, (3) **$60**
Right: **Jointed foil dressed devil with original wrap tag**
USA, 1950s, 14.5"H x 8"W, lightly embossed, (2) **$75**

Crawling baby
Germany
1920s
8"H x 7"W
heavily embossed
(1) **$650**
The apron is
hinged, giving this
exceptional piece a
pleasing 3-D effect.

Crows
Germany
1920s
7.75"H x 3.5"W
heavily embossed
Left: (3) **$100**
Right: (1) **$225**

Jointed foil skeleton with original wrap tags
USA
1950s
15"H x 8"W
lightly embossed
(3) **$50**

Arched-back cat
USA, Beistle
(no mark)
1930s
18.5"H x 11.5"W
lightly embossed
(4) **$50**

▼ **Trio of diecuts with original glassine envelopes**
Each envelope contains four identical diecuts
Germany ("Made in Saxony")
early 1920s, 6"H x 6.5"W
non-embossed
Left: **Witch,** (2) **$160 for set**
Middle: **Running JOL-man in suit,** (1) **$180 for set**
Right: **Black JOL with top hat,** (1) **$220 for set**

▼ *Left:* **Foil JOL with hat**
USA, 1950s, 13.5"H x 9.5"W
lightly embossed, (5) **$20**
Right: **Foil JOL with hat**
USA, 1950s, 8"H x 5"W
lightly embossed, (5) **$10**
Bottom: **Foil broomed witch** 5"W
lightly embossed, (5) **$20**

▼ *Top:* **Bat**
Germany
1920s
1.75"H x 5"W
heavily embossed
(3) **$60**
Bottom: **Bat**
Germany
1920s
3.75"H x 8.25"W
heavily embossed
(3) **$85**

▲ *Top Left:* **JOL pirate**
Germany, 1920s, 5.5"H x 5.5"W, heavily embossed, (2) **$70**
Top Right: **JOL with hat**
Germany, 1920s, 5.25"H x 5"W, heavily embossed, (3) **$40**
Bottom Left: **JOL with hair**
Germany, 1920s, 5"H x 5"W, heavily embossed, (3) **$40**
Bottom Right: **JOL with hair**
Germany, 1920s, 5"H x 5.25"W, heavily embossed, (4) **$40**

▲ *Top Left:* **JOL**
Germany, 1920s, 5.25"H x 5"W, heavily embossed, (5) **$30**
Top Right: **JOL**
Germany, 1920s, 5.25"H x 5"W, heavily embossed, (5) **$30**
Bottom Left: **JOL with hat**
Germany, 1920s, 5.5"H x 5"W, heavily embossed, (3) **$40**
Bottom Right: **JOL girl**
Germany, 1920s, 5"H x 6"W, heavily embossed, (4) **$35**

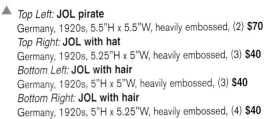

▲ *Left:* **JOL witch with cape**
Germany, 1920s, 7.25"H x 3.75"W, heavily embossed, (3) **$70**
Right: **JOL maid**
Germany, 1920s, 7"H x 3.25"W, heavily embossed, (4) **$70**

▲ *Left:* **JOL boy with diamond pants**
Germany, 1920s, 7.5"H x 3.5"W, heavily embossed, (3) **$65**
Right: **JOL clown**
Germany, 1920s, 7.25"H x 3.5"W, heavily embossed, (4) **$70**

▲ **Flapper JOL**
Germany
1920s
9.5"H x 11"W
heavily embossed
(4) **$55**

▲ **Pirate JOL with owl on hat**
Germany
1920s
10.25"H x 9.75"W
heavily embossed
(3) **$160**

▲ **Pirate JOL with skull & crossbones on hat**
Germany
1920s
10.5"H x 9.75"W
heavily embossed
(3) **$160**

▼ *Left:* **JOL witch holding broom**
Germany, 1920s, 7.75"H x 3.25"W, heavily embossed, (2) **$100**
Right: **JOL maid with starred clothes**
Germany, 1920s, 7.75"H x 3.5"W, heavily embossed, (3) **$80**

▶ *Left:* **JOL man with diamond pants and plain hat**
Germany, 1920s, 8.75"H x 3.75"W, heavily embossed, (2) **$140**
Right: **JOL maid with bangs**
Germany, 1920s, 8.25"H x 3.75"W, heavily embossed, (2) **$165**

DIECUTS

◀ **Black face JOL with printed transparency**
Germany
1920s
10"H x 11.75"W
heavily embossed
(1) **$700**
This exceedingly rare variation was almost certainly made for a single season only, and then in very small quantities. It may even be a discarded prototype.

◀ **JOL man with diamond pants**
Germany
1920–1930s
15.5"H x 7.25"W
heavily embossed
(4) **$55**
Many of the larger diecuts, like this one, came with easels.

▲ **Black face JOLs**
Germany, 1920s, heavily embossed
Left: 13.25"H x 15.75"W, (2) **$225**
Right: 10"H x 11.75"W, (2) **$185**

▶ **Crescent moon and cat**
Germany
1930s
13.75"H x 13"W
heavily embossed
(2) **$165**

◀ **Crescent moon and owl**
Germany
1930s
13.75"H x 13"W
heavily embossed
(2) **$165**

▲ **JOL with tongue out**
Germany, 1920s, 12.75" square, heavily embossed, (1) **$550**

▲ **Owl in tree**
Germany, 1920s, 12.75" square, heavily embossed, (2) **$375**

◀ **JOL maid with a black cat**
Germany
1920–1930s
15.5"H x 7"W
heavily embossed
(5) **$55**

▲ **Owl and Pirate**
Left: **Owl**
Germany, 1920s, 8.5"H x 4"W, heavily embossed, (3) **$55**
The tan-to-black coloring of this diecut was deliberate. Several black cat diecuts also have this same shading effect, likely an experiment done by the German manufacturers.
Right: **Pirate JOL man**
Germany, 1920s, 7.75"H x 3.5"W, heavily embossed, (3) **$75**

▶ *Left:* **Owl**
Germany, 1920s, 7.25"H x 3"W
heavily embossed, (4) **$40**
Right: **Owl**
Germany, 1920s, 7"H x 3.25"W
heavily embossed, (3) **$50**

▼ **Flying owl**
Germany
1920s
8"H x 11"W
heavily embossed
(4) **$65**

◀ **Flying owl with
large eyes**
Germany
1920s
10.75"H x 14.75"W
heavily embossed
(3) **$75**

◀ **Trio of owls**
Germany
1920–1930s
15.5"H x 6.5"W
heavily embossed
(4) **$60 each**

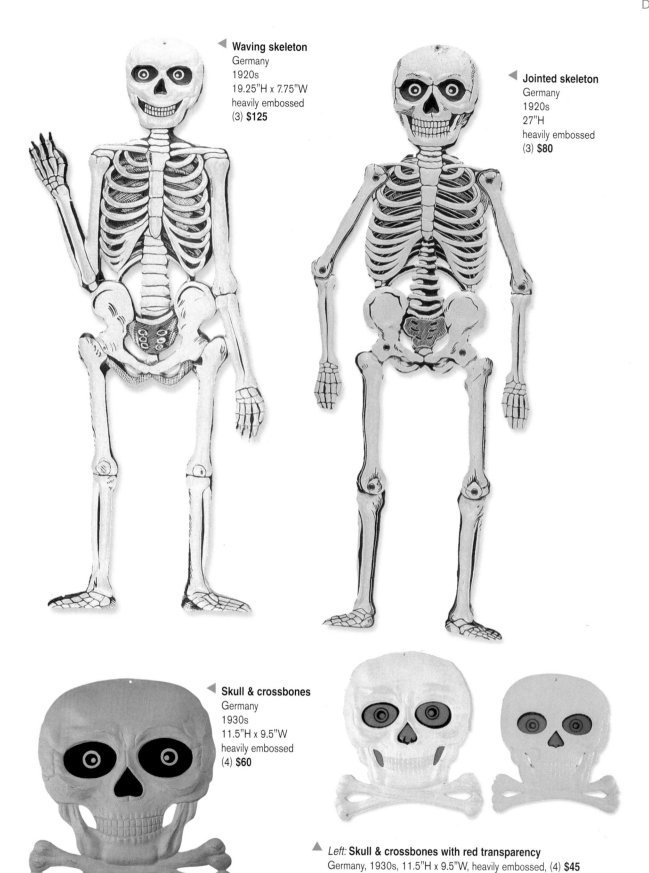

Waving skeleton
Germany
1920s
19.25"H x 7.75"W
heavily embossed
(3) **$125**

Jointed skeleton
Germany
1920s
27"H
heavily embossed
(3) **$80**

Skull & crossbones
Germany
1930s
11.5"H x 9.5"W
heavily embossed
(4) **$60**

Left: **Skull & crossbones with red transparency**
Germany, 1930s, 11.5"H x 9.5"W, heavily embossed, (4) **$45**
Right: **Skull & crossbones with red transparency**
USA, Beistle, (HE Luhrs mark), 1940s, 9.5"H x 8.25"W, lightly embossed, (5) **$20**

DIECUTS

193

◄ **Skull & crossbones
with hat**
Germany
1930s
10.75"H x 9.5"W
heavily embossed
(1) **$325**

► **Witch face**
Germany
1920s
6.5"H x 6.25"W
heavily embossed
(2) **$115**

► **Broomed witches**
Germany, 1920s, heavily embossed
Left: 7.75"H x 4"W, (4) **$50**
Middle: 8.5"H x 5.5"W, (3) **$65**
Right: 9.5"H x 7"W, (2) **$110**

▼ *Left:* **Broomed witch**
Germany, 1920s, 11.5"H x 11.75"W
heavily embossed. (3) **$75** It has an easel back.
Right: **Walking witch**
Germany, 1920–1930s, 7.75"H x 6"W
heavily embossed, (4) **$35**

▼ **Broomed witch**
Germany
1920s
16"H x 14.25"W
heavily embossed
(3) **$85**

It has an easel back.

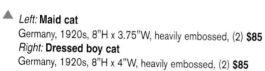

Left: **Maid cat**
Germany, 1920s, 8"H x 3.75"W, heavily embossed, (2) **$85**
Right: **Dressed boy cat**
Germany, 1920s, 8"H x 4"W, heavily embossed, (2) **$85**

Left: **Devil face**
Germany, 1920–1930s, 10.25"H x 9"W, heavily embossed, (4) **$85**
Right: **Witch face**
Germany, 1920–1930s, 13"H x 10"W, heavily embossed, (4) **$80**

▶ **Devil**
Germany
1920s
15.5"H x 6.5"W
heavily embossed
(4) **$95**

Left: **Waving cat**
Germany, 1920s, 7.25"H x 4"W, heavily embossed, (2) **$100**
Right: **Sitting cat**
Germany, 1920s, 7"H x 3.75"W, heavily embossed, (3) **$60**

▼ **Black cat face with hat**
Germany
1920s
5"H x 5.25"W
heavily embossed
(3) **$135**

▼ **Black cats**
Germany
1920–1930s
6.5"H x 4.75"W
heavily embossed
(5) **$35 each**

▲ **Devil faces**
Germany, 1920s, 5.25"H x 5"W, heavily embossed.
Left: (1) **$265**
Right: (2) **$195**

▼ **Black cats**
Germany
1920s
9"H x 7.5"W
heavily embossed
(4) **$65 each**

▲ **Devil with flame bottom**
Germany, 1920–1930s, 19.5"H x 8.25"W
heavily embossed. (4) **$100**
It has an easel back.

Left: **Black cat face with 13 teeth**
Germany, 1920–1930s, 7.75"H x 7.5"W, heavily embossed, (4) **$50**
Right: **Black cat face with 11 teeth**
Germany, 1920–1930s, 7.75"H x 7.5"W, heavily embossed, (4) **$50**

Black cat face with 14 teeth
Germany, 1920–1930s, 13"H x 13.5"W
heavily embossed, (2) **$185**

Seated black cats
Germany
1920–1930s
15.75"H x 6.75"W
heavily embossed
(4) **$70 each**

Black cat
Germany
1920–1930s
15.5"H x 11.5"W
heavily embossed
(4) **$55**

Left: **Black cat face with 12 teeth**
Germany, 1920–1930s, 10"H x 10"W, heavily embossed, (3) **$95**
Right: **Black cat face with 13 teeth**
Germany, 1920–1930s, 7.75"H x 7.75"W, heavily embossed, (4) **$50**

DIECUTS

◀ **Maid cat**
Germany
1920–1930s
15.5"H x 7"W
heavily embossed
(4) **$75**

◀ **Boy cat with checkered pants**
Germany
1920–1930s
15.5"H x 7.25"W
heavily embossed
(4) **$80**

▼ **Cat on a JOL**
Germany
1930s
14.5"H x 14.5"W
heavily embossed
(3) **$165**

▲ **Black cat couple**
Germany, 1920–1930s, 19.5"H x 8"W, heavily embossed
(5) **$100 each**
Both items have easels.

Cat with violin
Germany
1930s
15.5"H x 8"W
heavily embossed
(2) **$300**
This item has an easel.

**Cat with walking
stick waving**
Germany
1920–1930s
15.5"H x 7.25"W
heavily embossed
(4) **$95**

Cat with trombone
Germany
1930s
15.5"H x 7.5"W
heavily embossed
(2) **$260**

Cat with saxophone
Germany
1930s
15.5"H x 7.25"W
heavily embossed
(2) **$260**
This item has an easel.

▲ **An assortment of mini-diecuts. All have easels.**
Top Left: **Cat on JOL**
Germany, 1945–1949, ("USSR Occupied" on easel)
4"H x 4.5"W, heavily embossed, (2) **$175**
Top Right: **Cat by JOL**
Germany, early 1920s, 3.75"H x 5"W, heavily embossed, (2) **$195**
Middle: **JOL with hat**
Germany, 1945–1949, ("USSR Occupied" on easel)
4"H x 4.5"W, heavily embossed, (2) **$175**
Bottom Left: **Witch at cauldron**
Germany, early 1920s, 4.25"H x 4.5"
heavily embossed, (2) **$225**
Bottom Right: **Cat with sax-playing JOL girl**
Germany, early 1920s, 3.75"H x 4.5"W
heavily embossed, (2) **$195**

▶ **A set of mini-diecuts**
Top Left: **Boy devil with owl**
Germany, 1920s, 5"H x 2.25"W, heavily embossed, (1) **$275**
Top Right: **JOL clown**
Germany, 1920s, 5.25"H x 2.5"W, heavily embossed, (1) **$260**
Bottom Left: **Devil**
Germany, 1920s, 5"H x 2.25"W, heavily embossed, (1) **$275**
Bottom Middle: **Broomed witch**
Germany, 1920s, 5.25"H x 3"W, heavily embossed, (1) **$250**
Bottom Right: **Owl**
Germany, 1920s, 5"H x 2.25"W, heavily embossed, (1) **$230**

▲ **Complete set of small black cat band members**
From Left: **Cat with trombone**, Germany, 1920s, 7.5"H x 3.5"W, heavily embossed, (3) **$80**
Cat with bass, Germany, 1920s, 7.5"H x 4"W, heavily embossed, (2) **$95**
Cat with guitar, Germany, 1920s, 7.75"H x 4"W, heavily embossed, (2) **$95**
Cat with saxophone, Germany, 1920s, 7.5"H x 3.5"W, heavily embossed, (3) **$80**
Cat with violin, Germany, 1920s, 7.5"H x 4.25"W, heavily embossed, (3) **$85**
Cat with cymbals, Germany, 1920s, 7.5"H x 3.75"W, heavily embossed, (2) **$95**.

▲ **Complete set of small "Mickey Mouse" JOL band members**
From Left: **JOL with drum**, Germany, late 1920s, 7.5"H x 4"W, heavily embossed, (2) **$100**
JOL with saxophone, Germany, late 1920s, 7.5"H x 3.5"W, heavily embossed, (3) **$80**
JOL with drum, Germany, late 1920s, 7.75"H x 3.5"W, heavily embossed, (3) **$80**
JOL with horn, Germany, late 1920s, 7.75"H x 3.25"W, heavily embossed, (3) **$80**
JOL with accordion, Germany, late 1920s, 7.5"H x 4"W, heavily embossed, (2) **$100**
JOL with banjo, Germany, late 1920s, 7.75"H x 3.75"W, heavily embossed, (2) **$100**

◀ **Complete set of large "Mickey and Minnie Mouse" JOL band members**
Left: **JOL with horn**
Germany, late 1920s, 15.5"H x 6.75"W, heavily embossed, (3) **$135**
Middle: **JOL with cymbals**
Germany, late 1920s, 15.5"H x 7.25"W, heavily embossed, (2) **$160**
Right: **JOL with drum**
Germany, late 1920s, 15.5"H x 6.5"W, heavily embossed, (2) **$160**

DIECUTS

Complete set of small crescent moons. Production runs weren't always standardized. The crescent moons sometimes make up either the left or right sides of the diecut. These variations have no effect on the item's value.

Top Left: **Running JOL man** Germany, 1920s, 5" diameter, heavily embossed, (3) **$80**

Top Middle: **Bat** Germany, 1920s, 5" diameter, heavily embossed, (3) **$80**

Top Right: **Owl** Germany, 1920s, 5" diameter, heavily embossed, (4) **$70**

Bottom Left: **Seated cat** Germany, 1920s, 5" diameter heavily embossed, (3) **$80**

Bottom Middle: **Cat** Germany, 1920s, 5" diameter, heavily embossed (4) **$70**

Bottom Right: **Broomed witch** Germany, 1920s, 5" diameter, heavily embossed, (4) **$70**

Large crescent moon and broomed witch
Germany
1920s
10.25"H x 10.25"W
heavily embossed
(4) **$75**
Production runs weren't always standardized. The crescent moons sometimes make up either the left or right sides of the diecut. These variations have no effect on the item's value.

Left: **Large crescent moon and owl**
Germany, 1920s, 10.5"H x 9.5"W
heavily embossed, (3) **$75**

Right: **Large crescent moon and cat**
Germany, 1920s, 9.75"H x 9.55"W
heavily embossed (3) **$100**
Production runs weren't always standardized. The crescent moons sometimes make up either the left or right sides of the diecut. These variations have no effect on the item's value.

▲ Tiaras
Left: **Cat flanked by JOLs**
Germany, 1920s, 6.25"H x 9.75"W, heavily embossed, (2) **$225**
Bottom: **Clown JOL flanked by cat heads**
Germany, 1920s, 6.25"H x 9.75"W, heavily embossed, (1) **$350**
Right: **Owls flanked by stars**
Germany, 1920s, 5.5"H x 9.75"W, heavily embossed, (2) **$225**

▲ Tiaras
Left: **Witch and moon flanked by a cat and an owl**
Germany, 1920s, 6"H x 10.25"W, heavily embossed, (2) **$250**
Bottom: **Devil face flanked by cat heads**
Germany, 1920s, 6"H x 9.75"W, heavily embossed, (1) **$500**
Right: **Cat flanked by bats**
Germany, 1920s, 5.75"H x 10"W, heavily embossed, (2) **$200**

▲ Tiaras
Left: **Cat face flanked by bats**
Germany, 1920s, 5.5"H x 10"W, heavily embossed, (2) **$200**
Bottom: **JOL woman flanked by cats**
Germany, 1920s, 5.5"H x 9.5"W, heavily embossed, (2) **$235**
Right: **Witch face flanked by cats and JOLs**
Germany, 1920s, 6"H x 10"W, heavily embossed, (1) **$350**

▲ Tiaras
Top: **JOL pirate flanked by cats**
Germany, 1920s, 5.5"H x 10.25"W, heavily embossed, (1) **$650**
Bottom: **Cat with hat flanked by owls**
Germany, 1920s, 6"H x 9.75"W, heavily embossed, (1) **$650**

▶ **Jointed winged witch**
USA, Beistle
(no mark)
late 1920s
19"H x 19"W
non-embossed
(2) **$200**
This was
marketed as the
"Horrible Witch."

▲ *Left:* **JOL woman with broom**
Germany, 1920s, 19.5"H x 7.75"W, heavily embossed, (2) **$150**
Right: **JOL pirate**
Germany, 1920s, 19.5"H x 7.75"W, heavily embossed, (2) **$165**

These are the largest German diecuts seen. They were most likely used as store displays, which could account for their great rarity.

◀ **"Mickey Mouse" JOL playing saxophone**
Germany
1920s
26.25"H x 12.25"W
heavily embossed
(1) **$800**
This item has an easel.

◀ **Dressed cat playing banjo**
Germany
1920s
26.75"H x 12"W
heavily embossed
(1) **$900**

Jointed devil
lightning monster
USA, Beistle
(diamond mark)
1925–1930
29.25"H
non-embossed
(2) **$325**

Jointed "Bugs
and Wumpus"
lightning monster
USA, Beistle
(diamond mark)
1925–1930
29.25"H
non-embossed
(2) **$300**

Boxed set of 10 Halloween Cardboard Cutouts
USA, 1940s, 6"H x 7.25"W, (4) **$60**

Framed set of original
packaging for Beistle's
"The Dancing
Skeleton" and "The
Horrible Witch"
USA, Beistle
late 1920s
(1) **$225 each**

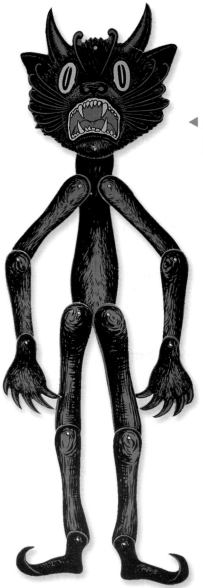

◄ **Jointed snarling cat monster**
USA, Beistle
(printed name)
1920s, 28.75"H
non-embossed
(1) **$400**

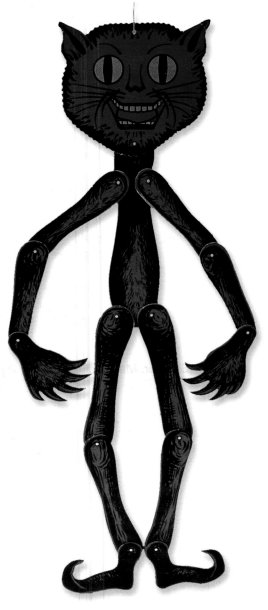

► **Jointed smiling cat monster**
USA, Beistle
(printed name)
1920s, 28.75"H
non-embossed
(2) **$300**

◄ **Hallowe'en Novelty Box containing multiples of a trio of different diecuts**
USA
late 1940s
7"H x 8.5"W
non-embossed
(2) **$125 set**

BIBLIOGRAPHY

Benjamin, Christopher. *The Sport Americana Price Guide to The Non-Sports Cards 1930-1960.* Cleveland, Ohio: Edgewater Book Company, 1993.

Campanelli, Dan and Pauline. *Halloween Collectables: A Price Guide.* Gas City, Ind.: L-W Publishing, 1995.

Fendelman, Helaine & Schwartz, Jeri. *The Official Price Guide: Holiday Collectibles.* New York: House of Collectibles, 1991.

Lasansky, Jeannette. *Collecting Guide to Holiday Paper Honeycomb: Cards, Garlands, Centerpieces and other Tissue-Paper Fantasies of the 20th Century; Oral Traditions Project of the Union County Historical Society.* Lewisburg, Pa., 1993.

Schiffer, Margaret. *Holidays: Toys and Decorations.* Atglen, Pa.: Schiffer Publishing, 1985.

Schneider, Stuart. *Halloween in America: A Collector's Guide with Prices.* Atglen, Pa.: Schiffer Publishing: 1995.

More Exciting Books From Krause Publications

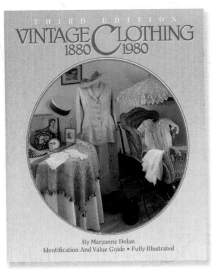

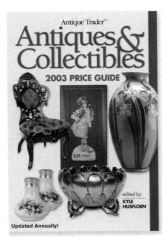
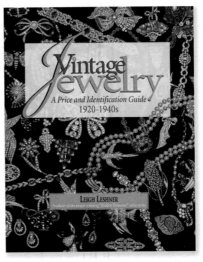